THE SINGING
JUNK-MAN

THE SINGING
JUNK-MAN

Stories of Grace and Hope and Humor

TRUMAN H. BRUNK

DreamSeeker Books
TELFORD, PENNSYLVANIA

an imprint of
Cascadia Publishing House

Cascadia Publishing House orders, information, reprint permissions:
contact@CascadiaPublishingHouse.com
1-215-723-9125
126 Klingerman Road, Telford PA 18969
www.CascadiaPublishingHouse.com

The Singing Junk-Man
Copyright © 2010 by Cascadia Publishing House.
Telford, PA 18969
All rights reserved
DreamSeeker Books is an imprint of Cascadia Publishing House LLC
Library of Congress Catalog Number:2010019819
ISBN 13: 978-1-931038-62-1; **ISBN 10:** 1-931038-62-7
Book design by Cascadia Publishing House
Cover design by Dawn Ranck

The paper used in this publication is recycled and meets the
minimum requirements of American National Standard for Information Sciences—
Permanence of Paper for Printed Library Materials, ANSI Z39.48-1984.1984

All Bible quotations are used by permission, all rights reserved and unless otherwise noted are from NIV taken from the Holy Bible, *New International Version*®. Copyright © 1973, 1978, 1984 International Bible Society. All rights reserved throughout the world. Used by permission of International Bible Society; NRSV from *The New Revised Standard Version of the Bible*, copyright 1989, by the Division of Christian Education of the National Council of the Churches of Christ in the USA; KJV from *The King James Version of the Bible*.

Library of Congress Cataloguing-in-Publication Data
Brunk, Truman H., 1931-
  The singing junk-man : stories of grace and hope and humor / Truman H. Brunk.
    p. cm.
  ISBN-13: 978-1-931038-62-1 (5.5 x 8.5" trade pbk. : alk. paper)
  ISBN-10: 1-931038-62-7 (5.5 x 8.5" trade pbk. : alk. paper)
  1. Christian life--Mennonite authors. I. Title.
  BV4501.3.B786 2010
  248.4'897--dc22
                                    2010019819

16 15 14 13 12 11 10   10 9 8 7 6 5 4 3 2

To our children and grandchildren:
Kathleen and Dean Isaacs and their children,
Andrew and Adrienne

and

Don and Deb Brunk and their family:
Isaac, Caleb, and Laura and their little ones

Contents

Introduction   11

PART 1: GUIDE MY FEET

1 Happy Am I with My Redeemer • 17
2 Sing a New Song (*Sermon*) • 19
3 The Mennonite Colony • 24
4 My Parents' Wedding Date • 26
5 No Hiding Place • 28
6 Selling Peaches in Williamsburg • 30
7 The Runaway Boy • 32
8 Grandfather Smith, Absentminded Professor • 35
9 The Old Black Bookcases • 38
10 Books Are Precious Friends • 40
11 My Grandfather George R. Brunk Sr. • 42
12 How Are You Related to George? • 44
13 When Brothers Disagree • 46
14 Don and Uncle George • 49
15 Remember the Sabbath Day • 51
16 Thou Shalt Not Buy Raffle Tickets • 53
17 Vic Victorious • 56
18 Stages of Faith (*Sermon*) • 58
19 What Goes Around Comes Around • 63
20 Dear Alice, Dear Joe • 65
21 Tom Schenk, Maverick Artist • 68
22 My Father's Eightieth Birthday • 71

23 All Aboard the "Pass Christian Victory" • 73
24 "Cowboys" Touring the Holy Lands • 77
25 Greystone Park • 80
26 An Unexpected Friend and Mentor • 83
27 The Best Storyteller of All • 85
28 Seminarians in Training • 87
29 Our Neighbor, Cousin Ivy • 89
30 The Gift of Grace (*Sermon*) • 91
31 The Gift of Sight • 98
32 Meeting at Harper's Ferry • 100

PART 2: DO JUSTICE, LOVE KINDNESS

Introduction 104
1 Do Justice, Love Mercy (*Sermon*) • 107
2 A Lenten Road Map (*Sermon*) • 110
3 All That I Have • 114
4 When Sam Calls, You Pay Attention • 116
5 Overhearing the Gospel • 118
6 Preachers' Kids • 120
7 The Best Seats in the House • 122
8 Jud Finds a Way • 125
9 North Meets South • 127
10 Not an Answer but a Presence • 129
11 The Gift of Affirmation • 132
12 A Letter from Liz • 134
13 My Bargain with Winfield • 136
14 Singing All the Way Home • 138
15 On Keeping the Main Thing the Main Thing • 141
16 My Friend Elmer • 142
17 Angels in the Pulpit • 144
18 Who's Afraid of Marriage Enrichment? • 146
19 Family Sculpting with Virginia Satir • 148

20 Finding Myself in Hot Water • 151
21 Continuing Education • 153
22 When the Heart Waits (*Sermon*) • 155

PART 3: LOVE MY SHEEP

Introduction 162
 1 Love My Sheep • 163
 2 Feed My Sheep • 165
 3 Sheep Pictures • 167
 4 The Meanest Service • 169
 5 A Trip to Remember • 171
 6 Renewal Through Baptism • 174
 7 A Note from the Other Side • 176
 8 Symbolic Gifts • 178
 9 Agape Class Retreat • 180
10 The Storms of Life • 182
11 How Many Pastors Does It Take? • 184
12 Interim Pastors, Temporary Shepherds • 186
13 Hello and Good-bye • 189
14 Read the Manual • 191

"One-Anothering" Sermons

15 Bless One Another (*Sermon*) • 194
16 Confess Your Sins One to Another (*Sermon*) • 200
17 Wash One Another's Feet (*Sermon*) • 206

Credits 211
The Author 212

Introduction

With the publication of *That Amazing Junk-Man* in spring 2007, the very first book signing took place at my home congregation, Warwick River Mennonite Church in Newport News, Virginia. It was the best book-signing experience anyone could ask for. Two sisters-in-law made the fellowship hall festive with fresh flowers. They served homemade pastries and hot tea.

We had sent a special invitation to family members of Preacher Taylor (who was indeed "That Amazing Junk-Man").

Heartwarming for all of us was the arrival of Preacher James Taylor's three daughters, a son, and grandson. Thressa (Taylor) Edwards and her husband Arthur came early and stayed late. They brought pictures to share. Next to arrive were her sisters, Naomi (Taylor) Francisco and Leoney Orie, Ernestine Taylor, their brother Samuel Lightfoot Taylor, and Jason Edwards, a grandson.

The first chapter in this second book, "Happy Am I," comes from the memories gleaned at that gathering and in the ensuing months. Since that day Thressa has kept in touch with us through phone calls and letters. We have learned much more about the Taylor family, especially "Preacher Taylor."

During my childhood and teen years I admired Preacher Taylor as a colorful preacher and a flamboyant "Junk-Man" who could walk into our orchard and climb the ladder and pick apples and throw them into the basket on top of his head without touching the basket. I did not bother to learn about his family. Our worlds were divided into black and white, far apart in the 1940s and 1950s.

Then in 2001 the folk opera, *Cross Tides,* was produced and presented at the Yoder Barn in Newport News, Virginia. Stories were gleaned from oral histories of "The Colony." A central character was James Taylor, friend, elder, preacher, and junk-dealer. The children and grandchildren of Elder Taylor worked with the producers, adding their stories. These were incorporated into the folk opera, and all of us learned things we had never known about this amazing Junk-Man and his family.

Steve Fannin, editor of *The Warwick River Tide* wrote in March 2001: "On opening night, John David Yoder welcomed the audience. He acknowledged family members of James Taylor . . . including twin infant great granddaughters [Kendyl and Keanna] with their parents."

Cross Tides provided a setting for the children of the Colony and the Junk-Man to learn to know each other. Children and grandchildren of Elder James Taylor filled roles alongside the children and grandchildren of the Mennonite Colony.

Regarding the opera, Thressa Taylor Edwards says, "They strove to bring out the truth of the era. . . . I don't think my father necessarily saw [the Mennonites] as white people. They were people he enjoyed being around. . . . We tend to bring in the black and white issue. To him that was not relevant."

From Thressa I learned that her father was born in Kingston, Jamaica, in 1902 (the same year my father was born) and came to Newport News in 1927. He married a beautiful woman, Carrie Rowe from Williamsburg, Virginia, and they raised eight children.

Preacher Taylor accepted Christ under the guidance of Elder Lightfoot Solomon Michaux, the "Happy Am I" radio preacher. (For a video of Elder Michaux preaching and singing see *YouTube—Elder Michaux—Happy Am I.*)

During about thirty years Taylor served as assistant pastor and field evangelist under Elder Michaux. When Michaux traveled to his other churches in Philadelphia and Washington D.C., Preacher Taylor was responsible to take care of the local church.

Thressa still attends the Church of God in downtown Newport News, where we young people from the Colony went to hear her father preach. When I asked her about the song "Happy Am I," I learned that the choir still sings the song, and she sent me the sheet music.

Thressa remembers her father returning home from his day's work and telling about his dealings in the Mennonite Colony. His children knew about our community and families, but we did not know much about his community and family.

In later years the Taylor family grew closer to the Mennonite church. Preacher Taylor's funeral was held on October 1, 1980, at Calvary Mennonite Church in Newport News, Virginia, where his daughter's husband, Leslie Francisco, was the pastor.

Now that you have read this Introduction, chapter 1, "Happy Am I with My Redeemer," will mean more to you.

You may also want to reread chapter 1, "We Called Him Preacher Taylor," in my previous book, *That Amazing Junk-Man* (Cascadia Publishing House, 2007).

Part 1
GUIDE MY FEET

1

Happy Am I with My Redeemer

The minute our own church service was over, we headed downtown.

Happy am I with my Redeemer,
Singing along the homeward way,
Happy am I, yes, happy am I.

The singing was lively, and these words were repeated over and over. All at once the minister, Preacher Taylor, raised his hands and stopped the singing. "Young white man in the back row, not clapping!" he said.

Me? I lifted my hands in front of my face and joined in the gospel song, clapping and singing along with the rest.

Going to Elder Michaux's church downtown was one of our favorite Sunday evening activities. We would try to slip into the back row and be as inconspicuous as possible. But sometimes he would spot us and say, "You young white folks, come on down here to the front," and there was nothing to do but follow the usher down the aisle.

One evening two carloads of us drove together to Elder Michaux's church. The minute our own church service was over, we piled into cars and headed to downtown Newport

News. We arrived about 9:00 p.m. and their evening service was just getting started.

First we heard testimonies by various members. More and more people arrived. Finally, the preacher entered and the congregation rose to its feet.

Preacher Taylor was one of several ministers at Elder Michaux's church, and he was the one we knew. He was the same Preacher Taylor who came to the Colony during the week, gathering up junk. We especially liked the times Preacher Taylor was the one to bring the message. He preached like a man inspired. His delivery was energetic, and the people responded with exuberant Amens.

One year we went to see the Easter pageant at Elder Michaux's church. For some reason, the program called for a dozen young women to walk slowly down the aisle to the front of the church and up onto the stage.

As one woman after another went front, the men in the congregation called out "Amen!" or "Hallelujah!" Sometimes it sounded like "Hallelu-YAH!" The prettier the woman, the louder the call. It was leading up to Easter—celebration time.

In later years, studying about worship at seminary, I heard Professor James Cone say that black worship is the closest thing to authentic worship. It is participatory. Testimony is integral to the service, as the believer stands before the community of faith and gives account of the hope that is in him or her. It involves heart, mind, soul, and emotion. It is true to Scripture.

But I had learned this truth many years earlier. No wonder we were drawn to the downtown church where we could clap our hands and move our feet and shout, "Hallelujah!"

Recently Betty and I have struck up a friendship with the daughters and a son of Preacher Taylor. Three of Preacher Taylor's daughters still attend the church we used to visit: Thressa, Ernestine, and Ivy. Thressa says the choir continues to sing a song, whose words and music she sent me, celebrating joy with our Redeemer who keeps our soul as we sing on our way.

2

Sing a New Song (*Sermon*)

She loved the singing but did not want to be preached at.

Text: Psalm 150

We decided to visit a neighboring church in our home community. We had noticed the sign that announced the topic of the morning, "Sing the Story," and we wanted to experience a morning of congregational singing.

Early in the service, the leader introduced a new song, "Nothing Is Lost on the Breath of God." He explained that the song was written after the death of a young child. While we sang, I noticed that the worship leader, sitting behind the song leader, had bowed her head and was wiping tears. And I remembered that she had lost a son in a construction accident.

The hymn by Colin Gibson included lines affirming that no creature or person is too small for God to seek and find.

I glanced at the couple sitting next to us. They too were wiping their eyes. They had lost a beloved daughter. And our whole community suffered. The words to this song could be a new "revised" translation of Romans 8:

"Neither height nor depth
nor anything else in all creation
will be able to separate us from the love of God
that is in Christ Jesus our Lord."

1. Music puts us in touch with our wounds.

It moves us to remember our own hurts
And reminds us of the grief and loss
We have experienced
as families
and as church families
and close communities.

There is power in listening to music alone.
But even more powerful
is the healing that comes when
a community experiences the music together.

God moves among us to bring healing.
We do not have to weep alone.
Brothers and sisters weep with us.
God weeps, too.

2. Music allows us to grieve.

"Does Jesus care," we sing,
amid life's losses and sorrows?
We are touched at the very center of life.
When we sing as one body,
gentleness, mercy, and tenderness come together.
Listening to music prepares the way for healing.

3. Music invites us back to God.

Anne Lamott, an author who lives in Northern California, writes about her search for God. In her book *Traveling Mercies*, she remembers her restless years as a young person.

On Sunday mornings
  She would find herself at a flea market
    feeling isolated and lonely.
  She would hear gospel music
    coming from across the street,
      from an old, dilapidated Presbyterian church.
  It was a ramshackle building,
    but the music was so pretty
      and she recognized the hymns.
  Finally, she began stopping by the church,
    and standing just inside the doorway
      to listen to the songs.
She always left before the sermon.
  She loved the singing
    but she did not want to be preached at.
She was "frozen and stiff"
  but the singing wore down all her defenses
and left her feeling soft and tender.

Anne made a new commitment to walk with Jesus.
The old church music brought her back to faith.

> *Back to life!*
> *Sharing God's joy,*
> *Full of mercy and grace,*
> *Bringing blessing and peace to others.*

No wonder we sing of our lives flowing on in "endless song" and of that light of the world who is Jesus.

4. Music links the generations.

Certain music carries us back to childhood. I remember my mother singing through the day. Anytime she was in the kitchen, she was singing in her high, soprano voice. She sang hymns, and she knew all the words. Later in life, in the nursing home, Mom was still singing. Sometimes while riding in her wheelchair, she would have the urge to sing.

One particular day,
I was pushing the wheelchair
    and Mom started singing "Amazing Grace."
I tried to hurry along to the outside patio
    where we could be alone with our singing,
but Mom was not as self-conscious as I was.
    Mom wanted to sing along the hallway too.
When I did not join in, she said,
    "Do you want me to sing the alto
        and you can sing my part?"

The day I worked on this sermon,
    I opened the August 21, 2007, issue of The Mennonite
        and noticed a picture of my young friend,
    Rachel Gerber, recent graduate
        of Eastern Mennonite Seminary,
            now a pastor at First Mennonite Church
                in Denver, Colorado.
    Rachel is holding her little son, Owen.
    She had written an article called "The Song of the Village."
    In it she describes the practice of
        a certain tribe in Africa:

Even before a child is born,
    the mother listens until she hears the song
        of her unborn child.
Then she teaches the song to her husband,
    and they teach it to the village.
While the baby is being born,
    the village surrounds the hut and sings this song,
which are the first words the child hears—
    who this child is and what he will become.

"The power of the song comes not only from listening
    but sharing it with others," writes Rachel.

We share the song so that
    one day, when the child forgets the words,
someone will be there to sing it to him again.

Don't all of us have a song to sing?

What keeps me from singing my song?
                  A timid tongue?
                  A wounded heart?
                  Deep fears?

Now is the time for my song to be sung.
Can I find the courage
    and strength
        and healing
so that I can sing my song?

Our praise, and our love,
    and our testimony
        are wrapped up in the song within us.
So let us pray for our song to be released.
    and pray that the song
        in our brother and sister also can be released
Until the whole world sings
    in worship and praise to our God.

> Sing to the Lord a new song,
>   sing to the Lord, all the earth.
> Sing to the Lord, praise his name;
>   proclaim his salvation day after day.
> —Psalm 96:1-2

3

The Mennonite Colony

*My roots go deep in the pine tree
groves along the Warwick River.*

Frequently I am asked, "What is the Mennonite Colony? Where is it? How did it get its name?"

Especially after the publication of my first book, *That Amazing Junk-Man* (DreamSeeker Books, 2007), I realize that it is necessary to address these questions. In that earlier book, here is the way I described my childhood home: "I grew up in the Colony. It was a Paradise, a walled garden. A hundred years before my time, pioneers traveled to southern Virginia from Ohio in search of good farmland. They found an old, run-down plantation with several thousand acres, bought it, and divided it into small farms."

Only in recent years has it dawned on me that the "Mennonite Colony" was named not by the residents but by the surrounding community. Located in southern Virginia where English settlers first named the counties and towns, there were the Jamestown Colony, the Yorktown Colony, and the Williamsburg Colony.

The Mennonite Colony was located on a peninsula near Warwick Courthouse, halfway between Newport News and Williamsburg. The mailing address was Denbigh. I have enjoyed reading Lillian Miller's privately published booklet, *Denbigh Daze: A Selection of Informal Writings,* in which she notes important dates and founders of the Mennonite Colony.

According to Lillian, Jacob Hahn from Michigan was the first Mennonite to bring his family to the area in 1897. She describes Hahn's original visit this way: "He took a few steps into the tall pine woods that surrounded the station, knelt down, and prayed for God to guide him in his selection of a home site. He hoped that the warm climate would help his desperately ill son."

Lillian notes that in February 1897 Daniel Shenk (my wife's grandfather) from Elida, Ohio, explored the area and then wrote a letter to a church paper describing the Williamsburg area and telling about special excursion rates the C & O Railroad was offering, inviting people to come and settle.

Mennonite men from Ohio, Indiana, Michigan, Pennsylvania, Maryland, and the Shenandoah Valley of Virginia came to see for themselves. A group met with Dr. John Young of the Young Plantation at Denbigh who had land to offer. They agreed to buy his 1,200 acres at $10.00 per acre. The plantation was divided into small farms.

By 1910 thirty families had arrived in the Colony. That year my grandfather George R. Brunk moved his family from Kansas. My father was eight at the time. Betty's father Daniel was six when he came to the Colony with his father, Daniel Shenk.

I have always loved hearing the stories of those early days. My roots go deep in the pine tree groves along the Warwick River. The Colony was a wonderful place to grow up.

4

My Parents' Wedding Day

*"There was no way to
get rid of him, so I married him."*

Because of the Great Depression of the 1920s, work was scarce all over America. Construction came to a standstill in Newport News, Virginia, where my father lived. Henry Brunk had left the Colony and established a building business in Washington, D.C.

Henry must have hired lots of Mennonite men from his hometown. Many of Dad's contemporaries traveled the four hours each week to D.C. and came home weekends to be with their families.

So at age twenty-one, my father left Newport News and found employment with Henry Brunk. He shared an apartment with Tom Schenk. We grew up hearing stories about the colorful life of these two young men living in the bustling nation's capitol.

From Washington, Dad made monthly trips to Elida, Ohio, to visit his fiancée, Ruth Smith. But winter 1922-23 must have been difficult, and Dad was having a hard time. His trips to Ohio were expensive, and his apartment-mate, who often rode along to visit his own family in Elida, would "forget" to pay his share of the gas. Dad was lonesome for his sweetheart, tired of doing his own cooking, and weary of supplying free transportation to his buddy.

The way Mom tells the story, Dad showed up at her home near Christmas that year and declared that he would not return to Washington without her. I've heard her explain, "There was no way to get rid of him, so I married him."

Grandmother Smith did her part. She and Aunt Beulah helped Mom make the wedding dress. Grandmother went with the young couple to obtain the marriage license.

The wedding party assembled in the home of Bishop John M. Shenk. Mom's sister Beulah was her only attendant, and Tom Schenk was Dad's best man. The attendants were the only guests. Afterward the wedding party went to Grandfather Smith's home for a small reception.

In later years, my father would tell the family about their first night together. They had traveled a ways, and it was late when they arrived at the motel. Just as they were settling in, Dad remembered the twenty-dollar bill tucked above the sun visor in the car. That was all the money he had, and he didn't dare risk losing it. So he put on shoes and coat and went to retrieve the money.

When he returned to the room, there was his bride, in her nightgown and robe, kneeling at the bed, praying! What to do? Dad said, "What could I do but join her?" So he knelt beside her and prayed, too.

When we would ask Mom about her courtship with Dad, she had to admit that Dad was "worldly." He wore a tie, he even smoked, and he was not too interested in spiritual things. But he was interested in her. I believe she was his path back to God, back to the church, and back to his family.

Mom was a holy woman. She took her faith seriously. When Dad was called to church work, Mom was behind him all the way. She was his encourager and cheerleader.

5

No Hiding Place

*Soon there was a growing
pile of sawdust on the parlor floor.*

Occasionally my parents traveled to the Knoxville Mission in Tennessee to have conversations with the mission superintendents, Homer and Katherine Mumaw. My parents had served at the mission for several years, and they continued to have interest in the work. On this particular trip to Tennessee, they took me along. I was five years old.

While the grown-ups met in the study, I was told I could play in the next room, called the parlor. The hosts gave me a wonderful toy carpenter set to play with. One of the little tools was a handsaw. I took that saw and wondered where I could use it. Looking around the room, my eyes came to rest on a goose-necked rocker with beautiful, shiny, curvy arms.

Without considering the consequences, I began to saw on one of those arms. The saw was nice and sharp. Soon there was a growing pile of sawdust on the floor.

The conversation in the next room seemed to be winding down. I became aware of my dilemma. Could I hide the sawdust? Could I hide the chair? Could I hide myself?

I remembered the words from the Bible Mom had taught me, "Be sure your sins will find you out." Already at the age of five, was I a sinner in need of redemption? I'm not sure anymore how this all worked out, but I am sure I was forgiven. It was there at the Knoxville Mission that I learned about grace and mercy.

I recall the old song we used to sing, "What can wash away my sin? Nothing but the blood of Jesus." To this day, I believe in the miracle of forgiveness.

6

Selling Peaches in Williamsburg

Our most illustrious customer was John D. Rockefeller himself.

"This tree marks the very spot where I sold peaches to John D. Rockefeller," I explain to my friends when I take them on a tour of Williamsburg, Virginia.

The historic cobblestone Duke of Gloucester Street stretches for exactly one mile linking William and Mary College to the Colonial Capitol building. Every chance I get I walk that mile-long stretch, remembering those hot August days of my boyhood. I like to pause under the elm trees and remember the blessed relief of their shade.

The magnificent old elm trees still line the street. I notice that one of the trees has died, and some of the others are looking not too healthy. The old cobblestones remain strong and solid. Enough landmarks remain so that my memory is refreshed.

Also jogging my memory is the photo in Mom's old photo album. It shows our 1935 Chevrolet completely covered with baskets of peaches. Peaches cover the hood of the car, reach all across the roof, and balance on the trunk at the back. What a picture! This was our showcase in the great open spaces of Duke of Gloucester Street.

When peaches ripened, we had to find ways to sell them as quickly as possible. Starting about the time I was nine years old, it was my assignment to go with Mom to Williamsburg to set up our peach stand. Tourists were good customers. They strolled leisurely along the street, sometimes stopping by our "showroom" to buy a basket of peaches and eat a few right on the spot.

Our most illustrious customer was John D. Rockefeller himself, the founder of Colonial Williamsburg. Mr. Rockefeller would make his way down the street in his top hat, carrying a walking stick and smoking a pipe. Sometimes he would stop and have a brief conversation with us and purchase a few of our peaches.

Southern Virginia is hot in peach season. I remember the "fancy lady" who came out of her house on the other side of the street and brought tall glasses of lemonade to Mom and me. She seemed like an angel.

Eventually, when I had my own driver's license, it was up to me to drive the pickup truck to Williamsburg and let Mom stay at home to take care of the customers there.

7

The Runaway Boy

My sister would be the first to admit that life with Al has not been boring.

The boy on the bicycle rode with determination. When he reached the James River Bridge, at that time known as the longest bridge in the country, he knew he had already come twelve miles.

He crossed the bridge and was in familiar territory near Deep Creek, Virginia, where his family had recently lived. He found his old house and it was empty. He decided to spend the night in his old bedroom.

Alvin had prepared for a long trip. On his bike he carried a sack of potatoes, a bag of cornmeal, dried milk, the big family Bible, and two dollars.

He untied the provisions and ate some of the potatoes. For breakfast he had cornmeal and dried milk. When he was ready to get back on his bicycle, he threw away the rest of the potatoes. They were too heavy and would slow him down.

He remembers the kindness of strangers. One man in Deep Creek told him that he knew a man who owed Alvin's dad some money. So he gave Al several dollars. A caring woman said, "I will give you enough money to pay the bridge toll so you can return across the bridge."

Back home Aunt Mary discovered that her nephew was missing. She telephoned the neighbors and called Brother Truman (my father) who consulted with the other preachers. They decided to contact the local policeman, Melvin Yoder, well-known in the community. They began to fit together the pieces to the puzzle.

Alvin's father and mother, Asa and Rebecca Hertzler, and five of their children had left the Colony and traveled to Florida where Asa had found work. During the Depression, families went wherever they thought they might make a living. They had left their oldest son living with his aunts.

When the police heard the story, they agreed with the preachers. They reasoned that, since Alvin was riding toward his parents, they should not treat this as an ordinary runaway case. They would not put out a missing persons bulletin for the thirteen-year-old boy.

Meanwhile, Alvin was making progress riding south on Route 17 through southern Virginia. When the sun went down he looked for a place to stay. He imagined warm sunny beaches and how he would surprise his parents when he finally arrived in Florida.

He remembers spending one night in a fire station. Several days into the journey, in New Bern, North Carolina, he stopped at a roadside store. When the owner realized where this young boy was heading, he told him that a truck heading south was expected in a few days. He suggested that Alvin wait and hitch a ride with the truck driver. A customer overheard the conversation and offered Al a place to stay until the truck arrived.

Alvin's bike was loaded onto the truck and traveling became easier. When they arrived in Florida, Al knew about where to locate his family. He found his dad working in a field. Together they went to the school to surprise his brothers and sisters. Then Dad took them all home to be reunited with Mom.

This story has a happy ending. Today we would be horrified if a child took off alone, heading for a destination a thousand miles away. Police would have issued an alert. Family would have been sleepless until the child was located. But in the 1930s some things were less sinister than they are now.

I have come to respect the word *contrarian,* defined as "a person who takes an opposing view, especially one who rejects the majority opinion."

I long ago decided that my brother-in-law Al would like to be labeled a contrarian. This is how he organizes his life. If you asked my sister Evelyn she might not always view this as a good thing. But she would be the first to admit that life with Alvin has not been boring.

8

Grandfather Smith, Absentminded Professor

He sat at his desk late into the night, reading, studying, and writing.

Most of the stories about my Grandfather Smith were told to me after his death. Some people called him "the walking encyclopedia of the Mennonite church." Others remembered him because of the many "absentminded professor" stories about him.

The account I have heard most often is the one that describes Grandfather talking near the fence with his neighbor. Grandfather said to the neighbor, "I'm not feeling well. I must be having a stroke." And the neighbor replied, "If you take your hands off this electric fence, you'll be all right."

Grandfather Jacob Brubaker Schmidt was born at St. Jacobs, Ontario, Canada, in 1870. When he turned twenty-one, his parents gave him the choice of a farm or a college education. J. B. chose education and this is the road that led to his life work in church colleges and pastorates. When Grandfather moved to the States, he adopted Smith as his family name.

My mother, Ruth Smith Brunk, told stories from the years when Grandfather Smith taught at Hesston College in Kansas. Grandfather loved the school, the students, and all the activities that go with being a caring teacher. His home was on the edge of campus and he enjoyed being part of campus life. Mom remembered seeing her father on Hesston's front lawn playing croquet with the students, forgetting to come inside at suppertime.

And Mom recalled her mother stretched out on the sofa, crying, lonely for her family back East, and depressed about the whole Kansas scene. Grandmother Smith did not love Kansas with its dust storms, the dry grassless prairies, the long days J. B. spent on campus. Mom remembered that things improved slightly when the family moved a little further from campus and her father spent more time with the family.

It must have been a relief to Grandmother Smith when J. B. was invited to Harrisonburg, Virginia, to serve as the first president of Eastern Mennonite School (now University.)

My mother told about the days of preparation when the family packed to leave Kansas to join the more conservative Mennonites in Virginia. Her mother made bonnets for all the girls. Before the train arrived in Harrisonburg, her father insisted that the girls put on their bonnets. Mom remembered the bonnets as huge and blue and that she and her sisters were most self-conscious. Blessedly, the hour of arrival was the only time they ever had to wear those bonnets.

My own memories of Grandfather Smith are from the days in Elida, Ohio, after his years in Virginia. Grandfather was a preacher and writer and a potato farmer. I remember him walking along the road in Elida pushing his potato cart. He labored hard during the day, raising and selling potatoes, then sat at his desk late into the night, reading, studying, and writing.

When the church suggested that members dedicate a parcel of land to grow vegetables and donate the proceeds to missions, Grandfather rented an acre of farmland for growing more potatoes. That's the crop he knew well. He called it "The Lord's acre."

One summer day, Grandfather bicycled out to the plot to weed the potato patch. He completed several rows before he began to feel heart pains. Help was summoned. His son Paul arrived in his car to take him home. A country doctor came to the house and prescribed bed rest. That night Grandfather died in his sleep.

When family members went to straighten his desk, they found his Bible open to the passage in Hebrews 13:14 KJV, "For here we have no continuing city, but we seek one to come."

9

The Old Black Bookcases

*My father had tried to
add a new coat of varnish.*

In my father's study stood three old black bookcases loaded down with all the Bible commentaries and other books that my mother and father owned. Many of the volumes were handed down from their parents. The whole scene gave the feeling of ancient history and serious study. As far as I was concerned, it was not a very inviting corner of the room. But when my father was in his eighties, he started asking, "When are you going to take the bookcases? They belong to you, you know."

I had known all my life that the bookcases were eventually supposed to be mine. I didn't want to think about it. They were impressive with their glass fronts which did a good job of keeping the books dust-free. But the wood was dark, almost black, and had a kind of gummy finish from the time my father had tried to add a new coat of varnish.

The day came when the family gathered to divide our parents' household belongings. We emptied the bookshelves and dissembled the bookcases. There were a hundred separate pieces, some fourteen inches square and some pieces as long as thirty-six inches. I packed the pieces into several boxes and hauled them to Pennsylvania where we were living.

By this time I had learned that the bookcases, which were joined together at the top and bottom, were called a barrister. Under the black gummy surface we found golden oak wood. On a fine spring day, Betty and I decided we would tackle this huge task of stripping and refinishing the wood. We each took one of the fourteen-inch squares. We worked all morning and accomplished very little. At this rate it would take years of Saturdays to finish this project.

Meanwhile, each time I drove to the church I passed a sign that said, "Furniture Refinishing." One day I stopped in to see the young man in charge of the business and showed him a piece of the barrister. He assured me that he could make this into a beautiful piece of furniture and gave an estimate for the cost. I decided it was well worth the money. If he did the work, at least it would get done in my lifetime.

Two weeks later, I stopped to pick up the finished product. The young man was proud of his work. He had uncovered the beautiful brass handles that now gleamed against the golden oak. He had found the date the bookcases were made (1899). They were unique antiques a hundred years old. They were works of art. I could hardly wait to install them in my home.

Now when guests come to our home, I like to take them to the corner of my study and show them the barrister bookshelves that once held the books of my Grandfather J. B. Smith, then the books of my parents, Truman and Ruth Brunk, and now hold my own collection. Someday I hope they will be an important part of our son's home, and maybe his son's. It looks to me like they could easily last another hundred years.

From generation to generation we will read and study and serve the Lord and tell the story of how God has redeemed us and made us his children.

10

Books Are Precious Friends

"I cannot live without books."
—Thomas Jefferson

These words of Thomas Jefferson appear on a little bookmark from a good friend of mine. The sentiment could be my own motto: I cannot live without books.

Books are treasures. Throughout my forty years in the ministry, I have attempted to read at least two books a week. Along with the Bible, the Best Book, my reading has provided the inspiration and energy needed for the constant preparation and planning that makes up the life of a pastor.

Some books stand out over time. Here are three volumes that I would not want to live without:

The Cost of Discipleship by Dietrich Bonhoeffer. "Jesus does not call us to come and dine but he calls us to come and die," Bonhoeffer observes. The emphasis throughout *The Cost of Discipleship* is that "cheap grace is the deadly enemy of the church. . . .We are fighting today for costly grace." Costly grace is the opportunity to follow Jesus, to do what it takes to please him, to suffer as he suffered and if necessary to die for him.

Bonhoeffer lived in difficult times. Hitler came to power and had to be resisted. Despite his pacifistic beliefs, Bonhoeffer stood up against Hitler and gave his life in the resistance to this ruthless dictator. Bonhoeffer's death was a fitting although troubling climax to a life of costly discipleship.

The Wounded Healer by Henri Nouwen. The title tells us what is coming. Jesus, the wounded healer, is our teacher. We are called to follow him and use our wounded places as we minister to others. Simple compassion and empathy grow out of the places we ourselves have been hurt and wounded.

Not only as wounded individuals, but we may be a whole company of wounded people following a wounded Lord. I need to come to terms with my own wounds and then convert my weakness and vulnerability into strength so that I can offer others the gift of healing and hope.

Exclusion and Embrace by Miroslav Volf. The writings in this book are authenticated by Volf's difficult life in the Balkans in the 1990s. He and his family experienced the horrors of ethnic cleansing. He watched as men in his family had their throats slit, and women were raped. Volf weighs how he can live in a world of such tragedy. He finally comes to the truth that Jesus taught—he has to forgive. In a day when many exclude the "other," Volf points to a God who opens arms to give us freedom.

As I grow older, it is a comforting thought that God waits for us with open arms, receiving all prodigals into his great house. Through Volf I have learned to live with God and also to live with the "other," who may be my opposite. Thank God for his non-remembering forgiveness. Volf's book is a testimony of grace.

Yes, books are precious friends. They enrich and bless and inspire my life.

11

My Grandfather George R. Brunk Sr.

Many people admired and almost worshiped him.

Stern, severe, dogmatic? Tender, caring, sensitive? How does one describe my giant of a grandfather? All of the above, I've learned.

I remember being afraid of Grandfather. If my parents had to go to church conference without children, they would sometimes leave us with Grandfather and Grandmother Brunk.

Is it really true or faulty memory? I seem to remember that Grandfather would find some reason to spank me soon after my arrival. Maybe he needed to show who was boss.

My sister Evelyn does not have this kind of scary memory. Evelyn has memories of fun times, loving attention, even a birthday celebration with a special gift. We agree Grandfather treated women in his household one way and men another.

So our grandfather evoked love and loyalty as well as fear and respect. Many people admired and almost worshiped him; others feared him and kept their distance.

In the Colony, where Grandfather was the bishop, both extremes and responses prevailed. My wife Betty remembers hearing her father, Daniel Shenk, quoting "Brother George." If Brother George said women were to wear long dresses and sleeves, then Betty's father would apply the rules in his home.

Years later, when we read the history of the Colony, it was eye-opening to learn that our other preacher, Daniel Shenk Sr. (Betty's grandfather), preached on God's love and grace. Betty wishes her dad would have sometimes quoted his own father's messages on love and grace and forgiveness.

So every other Sunday we would hear about grace. But the next Sunday, George R Brunk Sr. would preach on judgment.

I remember one Sunday at the end of his sermon Grandfather Brunk asked, "What shall I preach on next Sunday?"

The smallest man in our church cried out in a high-pitched, loud voice, "Brother Brunk, preach on hellfire!"

As I write, I have been trying to learn more about my grandfather. Grandfather Brunk was editor of the *Sword and Trumpet*, published quarterly, and self-described as "Devoted to the defense of a full Gospel, with especial emphasis upon neglected truths, and to an active opposition of the various forms of error that contribute to the religious drift of the times."

I cringe when I read Grandfather's harsh words about "drift" and realize how much of the time he stressed dogmatic "fundamentalism" while he decried "modernism."

In the *Sword and Trumpet*, all the various qualities of my grandfather can be seen and felt. I shed tears at the tender tribute he wrote for his foster son, Sidney. And I feel pride at Elder Michaux's letter telling of Grandfather preaching at his church.

At sixty-three, Grandfather died of a heart attack. My aunts and uncles tell how he tried to continue a normal life in his final years. Because of his weakened heart, at chore time he would crawl from the house to the barn, where he was found. It must have been a Wednesday evening, because our family was at church for prayer meeting. When we got the word, we rushed next door to his home. He lay on the bed, his body tended by my Aunt Esther. I was only six, but this memory remains vivid.

12

How Are You Related to George?

*Sometimes it takes an in-law
to get the family history sorted out.*

"How are you related to George R. Brunk?" This is the question most often asked of me when I meet folks across the church, especially at services attended by elderly Mennonites (and Amish).

After I reply that he was my uncle, I hear heartwarming testimonies of how Uncle George touched their lives. I respond proudly, "Yes, George and Lawrence were my uncles and Truman Sr. was my father."

Some years ago, after hearing so many questions about which Brunks I am related to—is it the Brunks in Washington, D.C., or the Valley of Virginia or the Brunks in the Tidewater area of Virginia—my wife figured out the answer. Have you noticed that sometimes it takes an in-law to get the family history sorted out? Her answer was partly in fun and partly serious, but it has worked for us:

"There are the Rich Brunks,
"and the Educated Brunks,
"and the Good-Looking Brunks,

"and the Big Brunks...."

"We are the Big Brunks!"

And that settles it, until the new acquaintance starts trying to figure out just who's who among the Brunks she or he knows.

Until a few years ago, we thought these four lines of Brunks were not related. Then somebody saw genealogies that go back to the 1700s and realized that all the Brunks are in fact related.

A friend sent me a clipping from the *New York Times* that was most interesting. I have tried to find more of this online and came up with this:

"Jonas Jonson Bronck (1600?-1643), also known as Jonas Jonasson Bronk, or Jonas Joanssen Bronck, was a Swedish immigrant to New Netherland after whom the New York City borough of the Bronx was named."

People would say, "We are going to the Broncks," and they were going to visit the Bronck family. That's how the Bronx got to be named the Bronx, or so the story goes.

13

When Brothers Disagree

Family members prayed earnestly for reconciliation, but nothing worked.

The whole family suffers when two brothers have a falling out. And when these two are well-known evangelists, the separation causes pain to many.

Uncle Lawrence was a successful businessman. During and after World War II he raised chickens and sold them on Jefferson Avenue in downtown Newport News, Virginia. I worked for him in the store, selling chickens to the African-American community. His slogan was: "Eat 'em any fresher and you eat 'em alive."

That slogan was typical of Lawrence. He was colorful, dramatic, mischievous, always creating a scene that got your attention. He was a lot of fun.

Lawrence was respected in the business community. Betty remembers when she was sixteen and a teller in the Bank of Warwick. Lawrence Brunk would come striding into the bank and walk past the teller windows straight back to the president's desk. The tellers stopped what they were doing. Everybody knew when Lawrence made the scene.

But Lawrence wanted to do more than make money. He had a dream that he and his brother George would join together in evangelism. George was the trained and experienced preacher, and Lawrence would provide the tent and equipment and trucks. They could combine their resources to form a team that would bring "the whole gospel to the whole world."

For five years the two brothers put all their energies into this tent evangelism. Aunt Dorothy and Aunt Margaret and all the children traveled with them from one town to the next. I remember when they were in Lansdale and Lancaster and Morgantown, Pennsylvania. I remember once they were in Oregon and my father got a call from them. They needed him to come to Oregon to mediate their differences.

There were other similar trips. Dad was on call whenever they needed him. Sometimes Dad would come home knowing that while the results of the mediation had pleased one brother, the other was not pleased with the outcome.

Finally the brothers decided they could no longer work together. Was it normal sibling rivalry? Was it ego? Was it theological differences? (This is what Dad called it.)

For thirty years the brothers stayed apart. Family members would try to intervene and bring about peace. Especially the four sisters in the family were determined to get the two brothers together. Family members prayed earnestly for reconciliation, but nothing worked. Matters seemed only to get worse.

The miracle happened when the brothers were in their eighties and my father in his nineties. Uncle Lawrence called from Florida and spoke with Uncle George, expressing a desire to reconcile. He was invited to come to George's home in Harrisonburg, Virginia, for a meeting.

On the way, Lawrence stopped by my parents' home in Newport News. I think Lawrence brought supper so they could eat together. Lawrence wanted Dad to go along to the Valley. But at ninety, Dad did not feel up to the four-hour trip.

Uncle Lawrence drove on to Harrisonburg and the two brothers had their meeting, made their peace, and embraced. Aunt Ruth (Brunk) Stoltzfus in her book, *A Way Was Opened,* describes the scene at the Calvary Sunday morning service held in Eastern Mennonite Seminary chapel.

> Following the sermon, George took Lawrence and Dorothy up front with him and soon asked Margaret to come up, too. George spoke first to pave the way for what followed. He mentioned the years he and Lawrence worked together in the Brunk Revivals, the years of estrangement that developed between them, and now the efforts toward reconciliation. Then Lawrence spoke. Dorothy and Margaret spoke. George and Lawrence embraced and kissed. It was a sermon in action. (p. 356)

Aunt Ruth asked Lawrence, "Why now?" and he replied that the alienation was too hard to bear, "It nearly killed me." And then he added, "In my old age I have learned to judge no one."

My father lived two more years after the reconciliation. It was a huge satisfaction to him to know that his two younger brothers had made peace.

14

Don and Uncle George

*I would never have wanted
this kind of public attention for our son.*

We heard that Uncle George, the evangelist, would be going to Pennsylvania on a special mission. He was to be a guest at Steve Wingfield's tent meetings and would symbolically transfer the "mantle of evangelism" to Steve.

I knew that our son Don was singing in the choir during this campaign. So when I saw Uncle George at a family reunion, I spoke to him. "You are going to be in our son's community tomorrow, I said. "Don will be in the mass choir. I know he will want to meet you after the service. Could you give him a blessing too?"

Don is an inspiration to me. Despite a heavy work load (in the building business), he is always giving high priority to the work of his local church. He enjoys working with youth; he leads contemporary worship; he sings in the choir; he leads a prayer ministry. And more!

Little did I know what this conversation with Uncle George would lead to. Don called late Sunday evening, saying, "Do you know what happened tonight? Uncle George had a ceremony of handing the mantle of evangelism over to Steve. Then he stayed at the podium and called out, 'Is Don Brunk somewhere in our audience? If so, come on up here with me. Your dad wants me to give you a blessing!'

"Shaking, I made my way from the choir loft to where Uncle George was standing. He said, 'Kneel!' Then he laid his hands on me and blessed me."

I would never have wanted this kind of public attention for Don. When I had made the request, I meant that it would be nice if Uncle George and Don had a personal conversation after the service in which Uncle George acknowledged Don's interest in the church and maybe offered special words of encouragement and blessing.

Upon hearing this description of what actually happened, I was alarmed. Was Don embarrassed? Did he think I was out of line to ask this favor of Uncle George?

I need not have worried. Don was elated. He felt truly blessed! He sent me a video of the whole evening, and it included this segment of the service. Don received a blessing from his uncle. It was a special, unforgettable moment.

15

Remember the Sabbath Day

If I accepted their candy, would I be guilty of sin?

God created the earth in six days and on the seventh day he rested. And this was to be the pattern in my parents' home. Our family attended church services Sunday morning and evening. We came home to a delicious Sunday dinner at noon.

After dinner we were expected to find holy things to do: read a missionary story or read from the big Egermeier's Bible Story Book. (Dad gave me fifty cents every time I read through the book.)

We were allowed to have friends over for the afternoon, and sometimes we went to visit other families. But our activities were limited. No ball games, no swimming in the river, no skating. We were to be quiet.

I remember the Sunday when Dad let me walk the mile to Michael's house. I was halfway there when three teenage boys in a Model A Ford stopped and offered me a ride. They were some of the rowdy young fellows from church, and I rather admired their free spirits.

They opened the door and I climbed in. One of the boys offered me a candy bar. They had a whole bag of candy bars and I could tell they were coming from the corner store. They had bought the candy on Sunday!

These boys were just a few years older than I, and had the same training I had. Like me, they had learned to sing, "We must not work on Sunday, Sunday, Sunday. We must not buy on Sunday, Sunday, Sunday because it is a sin."

I was uncomfortable. If I accepted their candy, would I be guilty of breaking the Sabbath? I turned down the offer and rode in silence the half-mile to Michael's house.

Today we live in a different world. After church, we often meet friends for lunch at a local restaurant. When we get home, there is the whole afternoon for sleeping, watching football, or getting together with family. We might even go to the grocery store if we have an urgent need for one or two items.

On Sundays I remember the rules of my childhood, and I like being free from those rules. But I do want to honor the Sabbath. I need to do some reflection on this and come up with something creative and positive so that this day is not like every other day. Maybe I will take this to my small group for discussion.

16

Thou Shalt Not Buy Raffle Tickets

Levi and Amanda decided to maintain their church membership and their poverty.

I remember a conversation that took place in my home when I was about five years old. It made a powerful impression that stays alive in my memory all these years later.

If church discussions took place in our home, they usually happened in my father's study with the door closed. But this conversation took place in our living room. My parents must have thought I was too young to be paying attention.

Several deacons and my father were talking with a family friend, also a member of the church, Levi Shenk. The decision was being made to take some sort of action against Brother Levi.

Levi lived in the Mennonite Colony but operated a place of business in the middle of a poor neighborhood in Newport News, Virginia. He drove the twelve miles each day to his store on Jefferson Avenue, where he sold packaged coal to families in the area. He also had washing machines where families could bring their laundry. It could never be called a flourishing business, but this was the way Levi and Amanda provided for their family.

Levi's customers were poor people, and Levi and Amanda were poor. Levi was well-known in his business community for being honest and fair, and he tried to be generous. So one day when one of his customers came into the store asking for donations to a worthy cause, Levi gave her a dollar. She in turn gave him a raffle ticket. Levi thought he was making a contribution, but when she handed him a ticket-stub he accepted it and put it in the till.

If that had been the end of the story, Levi would not have been in trouble with the church. But it was not the end of the story. Levi had the winning ticket. He was declared the Big Winner. He had won a race horse!

The family celebrated! A race horse worth thousands of dollars! It was estimated to be worth between ten and fifteen thousand dollars, a huge amount of money in those days.

If they could sell the horse, the family could pay off some debts. Maybe they could even make a down payment on a house. With seven children, there was plenty of excitement and lots of dreaming about how the money should be used.

But wait. When the church leaders heard the news, they called together the group who were now in our living room. Although Levi had contributed to the neighborhood cause, when he accepted a ticket, he was gambling. Gambling is sin. Levi would be asked to return the horse and confess his sin. Or he would lose his membership in the church.

Of course Levi wanted to keep his good standing in the congregation. He did as he was asked, gave the horse back, and humbly stood up in church to make his confession.

Recently I talked with my friend, John, youngest son of Levi. Together we reflected on how powerful the church was in our lives. Our church tried hard to be faithful, nonconformed to the world, living as followers of Christ, caring for each other, and confronting each other.

There was no way Levi would have agreed to forfeit his church membership. John remembers what a difficult time this was for his sisters and brother. They watched their parents make the decision to maintain their church membership and their poverty.

I think of John's five sisters and one brother, Mildred, Mary, Margaret, Miriam and Martha, and Lester. All of them made a rich contribution to the life of the Colony and to the surrounding community and to the wider church.

John remembers that shortly before his father's death Levi told his son that his last years were his best. John heard Levi say, "Why did it take so long for me to know how to live and to enjoy the good life?"

17

Vic Victorious

The orphanage houseparents drove to the Colony to pick him up.

A staff member from the local high school called our home in the middle of the afternoon. "Somebody is here in the office who wants to come to see you and he doesn't want me to say who it is. Are you at home and can he come?"

I don't like surprises or guessing games much, but how could I turn down this person who wanted to visit me? So I replied, "Yes, send him to the house." Betty and I cleared the coffee table of newspapers and empty cups and got ready for our mystery guest.

Five minutes later a van with an Ohio license plate drove in the lane. I stepped out to greet the couple walking up the sidewalk. The man was as tall as I am. He reached out his hand and said, "Do you remember me?"

There was something familiar about him, but no name came to mind. I asked, "Were we in high school together?" When he answered, "No, it was before that," I asked, "Are you Victor?"

I often remembered the way Victor disappeared from our fifth-grade class. One day he was there; the next day he was gone. Our teacher was unable (or unwilling) to answer our questions about what had happened to Victor. Even at home I could not get a satisfactory answer about why he was no longer at school.

Some of Victor's older siblings came to our church. Eventually I found out that he was living in a children's home in Ohio. I learned that his mother had died and his father and older siblings were barely able to keep the home together. Apparently the church leaders had helped the family make the decision to send Vic to Adriel School in the Mennonite community at West Liberty, Ohio. There he would receive the care and attention and guidance needed by a ten-year-old boy.

During this recent visit in our living room, I learned "the rest of the story." Victor (now called Vic) explained his last day in our home community, as the houseparents at the orphanage drove to the Colony to pick him up. He described standing in my parents' driveway and my father opening his wallet and handing Victor a dollar bill. That dollar bill somehow gave him courage and hope for the long journey ahead.

The best part of the visit with us now was learning what a healthy survivor Vic is! Not just a survivor, but Victorious! Vic says the move to Ohio was the best thing that could have happened to him. His houseparents brought discipline into his life, encouraged him in his schoolwork, and urged him to go to Goshen College in Indiana. He made wise choices along the way. He has an attractive wife who is his loving companion and coworker.

In the years ahead, I hope to spend time catching up with Vic and Bev. I know they are giving their retirement years to volunteer service. They have worked with Mennonite Disaster Service (MDS), with mission boards of the church, and with Habitat for Humanity. They volunteer wherever they see a need.

I thank God for Vic and for the life he has lived. And I am thankful that he chose to look me up and share "the rest of the story" about my missing classmate.

18

The Stages of Faith (*Sermon*)

*Each new ring is
added to the previous rings.*

Text: 2 Peter 3:18. "Grow in the grace and knowledge of our Lord and Savior. . . ."

It is my desire to keep on growing in faith, and to encourage the continued growth of those around me. An important book by John Westerhoff offers insight that helps me understand my own faith development and the faith development of those with whom I work. In his book, *Will Our Children Have Faith?* Westerhoff refers to the growth rings of a tree:

    1. A young tree with one ring is whole and complete with its one ring.

    2. A tree with many rings is a more expanded tree, but this does not make it a better tree.

    3. In a healthy environment, a tree grows and adds rings.

    4. A tree adds one ring at a time. It does not grow from a one-ring tree to a three-ring tree.

    5. As a tree grows, it does not eliminate rings. Each new ring is added to the previous rings.

I believe that each ring, and each stage of faith, is important in our conversion experience. Here are some ways to think of four rings of faith. Picture in your mind the central ring, adding each new ring as faith matures.

1. Experienced Faith (Infant)

The inner core of faith forms as a child interacts with parents and caregivers. The child experiences trust, love, and acceptance. The way a child is held and cuddled, parent-child eye contact, the touch of blessing, the sound of a loving voice that affirms and encourages—all these build faith in the child.

Trust, love, and acceptance are important to Christian faith. When these are missing, then loneliness and pain are built into the infant's life—a poor core on which to grow strong faith.

2. Dependent Faith (Ages 3-11)

If the needs of the first stage have been met, the child opens heart and mind, trusts parents and teachers, and drinks in their offerings. Faith grows as the child hears the Bible stories:

Adam and Eve in the garden,
Noah's ark,
Baby Moses in the bullrushes,
Joseph and his coat of many colors.

For me, these were the years spent among the green curtains of Sunday school, in the church basement, when I was being filled with faith stories and blessed by holy teachers.

I loved going to church. I looked forward to seeing Amos Brenneman in his big, baggy coat with bulging pockets that held candy for the children. I loved meeting Michael and Mabel, Peggy, Estelle and Leona, Esther Mable and John Henry. We were little brothers and sisters learning about God and church and our big world.

3. Searching Faith (Youth Questioning)

Some of us have never had the benefit of an environment that encouraged searching faith. During this stage, young people begin to ask hard questions. What had been received so uncritically must now be pulled out for investigation and experimentation. Their questions often make parents and teachers uncomfortable. They might ask,

"Who am I?"
"What do I believe?"
"What can I base my life on?"
"How do I construct a faith true to who I am?"

Some persons leave the church during this stage. What they need is a faith community that allows, even encourages, their intellectual struggles. Somewhere amid all these questions, the young person is called to commitment and baptism.

We need to make clear to the young person that baptism is not the *end* of faith development. Baptism is the *beginning* of a long journey and the questions will be a part of our faith formation as long as we live!

4. Owned Faith (Youth Maturing)

This movement from experienced faith and dependent faith through searching faith leads to the fourth stage when we are able to say, "This I believe." We learn to stand up for our beliefs and commit ourselves to putting our faith to work.

In the previous stages of faith, there seems to be a strong component of personal salvation. In finally claiming our own faith, we become aware of the needs of others. A person coming into owned faith might ask for a list of openings where one can go to feed the hungry, heal the sick, or visit the destitute.

A person who has come to mature faith might want to forget or ignore the earlier rings of faith. But, like the tree, the earlier rings are still part of the whole: the characteristics of dependency and the hard questions of searching faith will always be there. The faith journey will contain all the stages of growth.

We need to provide the safe and nurturing environment where all of us, young and old, can continue our faith pilgrimage and enjoy steady growth as we add rings of faith to our belief and understanding.

To me the rings of faith make a lot of sense. When I study Scripture, and when I sing the songs of faith, I often think of these rings of development. Let's consider some songs and Scripture for each ring:

1. Experienced Faith

In John 1, the disciples found in Jesus a loving, compassionate, patient friend who cradled them in the bosom of faith. The disciples asked, "Master, where do you live?" Jesus replied, "Come and see."

Songs might be: Lullabies
"Away in a Manger"
"Jesus Loves Me, This I Know

2. Dependent Faith

In Matthew 5 the disciples were always pushing to get into the picture with Jesus. They drank in his love and his message. In verses 1 and 2 the disciples came to Jesus and he taught them saying, "Blessed are the poor in spirit, for theirs is the kingdom of heaven. Blessed are the. . .; Blessed. . . ."

Songs might be: "This Little Light of Mine"
"Tell Me the Stories of Jesus"
"I Want Jesus to Walk with Me"

3. Searching Faith

In Mathew 16, Jesus asked the disciples, "Who do people say that I am? Who do you say that I am?" Jesus invites them to journey to Jerusalem with him. There is trepidation and fear, and finally there is following!

Songs might be: "Guide My Feet"
"Lord, I Want to be a Christian"
"When the Storms of Life Are Raging, Stand by Me"

4. Owned Faith

This has to be Pentecost! In Acts 2:4, the believers were in one place, and waiting. "All of them were filled with the Holy Spirit." This is the language of inclusion, opening our circle to include others. This is the language of "across the street and around the world." The language of hospitality!

Songs might be: "Eternal Father, Strong to Save"
"The Church's One Foundation"
"God of Grace and God of Glory"
on thy people pour thy power."

Another line from this last hymn says: "Grant us wisdom, grant us courage, for the living of these days."

Once again 2 Peter: "Grow in the grace and knowledge of our Lord and Savior Jesus Christ."

Amen.

19

What Goes Around Comes Around

*I moved my ladder as
close to Dad's as I could.*

My son Don and I were painting the house that summer. It was a long, hot job. But if we planned right, we could work on the shady side without too much discomfort.

We usually placed our ladders a few feet apart and could easily communicate while we slapped on the paint. But I remember one day that I kept trying to move my ladder away from Don, and he would quickly move his ladder so that we were once again within talking distance.

He was wearing me down; he just wouldn't give up. He needed a car, he said. He needed to go out with his friends. He needed to not be dependent on Mom or me; he needed his independence!

I was transported back to an earlier time. My father and I were picking apples. Our tall ladders were placed on the same side of the tree. But I noticed that Dad kept getting away from me, moving his ladder to the other side of the tree. I would quickly pick the apples at my location, then drag my ladder to where I could continue a rather one-sided conversation.

And that conversation was all about motor scooters. I must have been fourteen, and we had a bumper crop of fruit. I thought there was likely enough money in my father's account that he could grant my wish.

World War II was over. New cars were appearing in the church parking lot. Most things that had been rationed were now readily available. Gas was no longer in short supply.

I was consumed with the wish for a Cushman motor scooter. I had seen the scooter of my dreams in the window of Tidewater Motors in Newport News.

Day after day I moved my ladder as close to Dad's as I could. I must have worn him down, because finally one day he said, "Let's go look at the motor scooter."

I was elated! Dad wrote the check for $300.00 and the motor scooter was mine! All the way home, I was floating on air. As soon as we arrived home, I was on the road on that Cushman. The Colony roads belonged to me. I could go anywhere, anytime, without having to wait for a grown-up to take me.

Now I wonder where all those Cushman motor scooters have gone. I do know that eight of them are parked, in pristine condition, in Norman Good's garage. They must think they are in motor scooter heaven. (Norman is a retired businessman and friend from our days at Blooming Glen in Pennsylvania.)

When he turned eighteen, Don finally got a car to call his own. His persistence finally paid off. He took over one of the family cars, a 1973 Toyota Celica, and drove it until he was out of college and could afford a newer model.

20

Dear Alice, Dear Joe

*Thousands of refugees were
dying for lack of food and clothing.*

A friend gave me a book to read entitled *Dear Alice*. Soon I realized that the setting of the book was my home community of Denbigh, Virginia. The letters were written by Joe Brunk to his young wife, Alice Yoder Brunk. Joe and Alice's grandson put the book together. Here's how the story unfolds:

Joe Brunk from Goshen, Indiana, and Alice Yoder from Denbigh, Virginia, were married in the early 1900s. Early in their marriage they moved to the Mennonite Colony in Denbigh and set up housekeeping near Alice's parents.

By 1920, two little sons had joined their young family. Times were hard, food was scarce, and luxuries were nonexistent. Like all the Colony neighbors, Joe and Alice had their own vegetable garden to keep their family fed. A large portion of the garden was reserved for growing potatoes.

One day, the story goes, Joe spent the whole day weeding the potato patch. While he worked he pondered the news he was hearing about the hungry people in Europe. Thousands of World War I refugees were dying for lack of food and clothing.

Joe came into the house that evening with a heavy heart. He had heard that church people in America were starting to send food and clothing and workers to Turkey. The Mennonite churches were establishing the beginnings of Mennonite Central Committee (MCC) and needed volunteers to go and be the "hands and feet of Christ."

Joe told Alice that he couldn't get these things out of his mind. He wondered if God might be calling him to go to Turkey to help in some way.

Joe must have spoken with conviction, because his wife seemed to understand and gave her support to his call. Both of them knew it would be a difficult year. But Alice had family close by. She was confident that they would help her with the boys.

Joe soon left for his MCC assignment in Turkey. The young couple wrote letters weekly, Joe telling Alice of the hardship and death he witnessed in Europe and Alice writing about family life and their growing boys.

It was a gripping book. I could not lay it down. Surely this young man had placed himself amid the Lord's urgent work. Then I came to the last chapter titled, "Grandpa and the Tyrant." To my dismay, I read the painful notes written by Ivan Brunk about *his* grandfather and *my* grandfather.

Joe Brunk had moved to the Colony from Goshen, Indiana, where he had been employed by Goshen College. Even though Goshen College was sponsored by the Mennonite church, young people from the Colony were not encouraged to attend Goshen because of its western, more "liberal" ways.

If young persons went to college at all, they were expected to go to the new Eastern Mennonite School in Harrisonburg, Virginia. There traditional Mennonite values were closely aligned with Colony Mennonite beliefs and practices.

Since our leaders did not appreciate the "worldly" views of Goshen College, Joe's attendance there made Joe suspect from the first. Now Joe had joined the work of Mennonite Central Committee, also thought of as worldly by Colony standards.

These alignments (Goshen College and MCC) were more

than the leaders in the Colony could handle. Joe was not to be mentioned in the pulpit or prayed for in the public prayers.

At no time during Joe's year in Europe was his absence even acknowledged by his home congregation! Week after week Alice sat in the church service knowing that she and her husband and family would not be prayed for!

No wonder Ivan Brunk called the last chapter "Grandpa and the Tyrant"! After I finished the book, I thought to myself, with all this Denbigh history, it's too bad this wonderful book cannot be in the Warwick River Church library. The members would have loved the book, but would have felt disloyal reading all these negative reflections in the last chapter.

Imagine my surprise when I next visited the church at Denbigh. Right there in the library, placed in an honorary position, stood *Dear Alice*. I said to the librarian, "I'm surprised to see this book here, with all the negative things written in the last chapter." She replied, "Oh, we just cut out that chapter."

And sure enough, the last dozen pages had been carefully removed from the book.

21

Tom Schenk, Maverick Artist

I wonder if anyone ever offered to baptize Tom down by the river.

Tom Schenk was a colorful character. He was an artist, a friend, and a relative through marriage. He is the only person I know who attended the weddings of both my parents and my wife Betty's parents.

All my life I had heard stories about this colorful Tom Schenk. When my dad told them, the stories were usually connected with some prank or joke Tom played on his friends.

Then when I was in my forties, Tom came into my life out of the blue. How often does it happen that your parents' close friend becomes your own friend? By now he was seventy years old but still very much alive with a quick sense of humor and the desire to tell long tales. I started to hear faintly familiar stories my dad had told. This time I heard them from a new and different angle—Tom's angle.

All his life Tom wanted to be an artist. His parents did not understand this desire, and his church community also did not know what to do with this dream. He says they would have been happy to have him paint barns and houses, but not to paint portraits. So all his life he was a "rebel," his occupation not blessed by the church.

Many of his stories had to do with his disconnect with the church. He was quick to joke that he had been thrown out of every one of the Mennonite colleges. From his telling, I could see why he did not last in any institution that had rules.

But by the time he was seventy years old, he was being "discovered" by church institutions. He was commissioned to paint four of the founding Anabaptist martyrs of the sixteenth century. He used current Mennonite leaders as the models for the portraits. These original portraits hang in the meeting room at Laurelville Church Camp in southwestern Pennsylvania.

After he painted the martyrs, he was commissioned by Eastern Mennonite College to paint the presidents of the college. These originals hang in the historical library at Eastern Mennonite University.

As he made his reentry into the church community, Schenk's work appeared in Mennonite denominational publications, and he came back into circulation. He was commissioned by friends to paint portraits of family members. He made frequent trips through the Shenandoah Valley, connecting with clients and delivering his most recent work.

I believe that Tom was proud of this reconnection to the church. But he could not resist telling stories of the period in his life when he and his friends were trying to discard all things Mennonite.

Many of his stories included my father. For instance, Tom remembered walking with Dad over the Potomac River, standing in the middle of the bridge, and my dad pitching his plain coat over the rail. On the way to the river, the arms of the coat filled with air so that once it hit the water, the coat floated like a balloon down the river, with the arms waving good-bye.

In the early 1920s, Tom and my father shared an apartment in Washington, D.C., where they found employment during the Depression. My father left the apartment for a few hours and came back late at night.

During his absence, Tom had changed the living room furniture all around. When Dad opened the front door, he thought he was in the wrong place, quickly closed the door, and walked up and down the street trying to figure out which door belonged to him. Tom would laugh so hard he could barely finish the story.

When Tom told a story, he painted pictures for your imagination. Tom said he believed church rites should be something one could reproduce in a painting. He thought baptism through pouring was not artistic. He could not imagine being baptized in the front of a church, with the bishop pouring water on your head. Baptism in the river would be an authentic picture.

I wonder if anyone ever offered to baptize Tom down by the river. I wish I would have thought of giving such an invitation. I believe he would have agreed.

22

My Father's Eightieth Birthday

*The checkout woman stood on
tiptoe and planted a kiss on Dad's cheek.*

Our family has fun remembering the last years in the life of our father, Truman H. Brunk Sr. If ever a person aged graciously, it was our dad. And somehow he invited the grace of those around him. People loved to take care of Dad and show him special kindnesses. He would tell these happenings at family gatherings.

Most of the time when Dad left the house, he wore a black suit jacket or a black overcoat. With his tall stature and extra-large build and his slowing gait, he did look the role of a retired churchman.

Almost every day Dad left the house to drive a mile to the nearest grocery store. Any small item mentioned by Mom would propel him to his old Mercury and out of the house.

On December 23, 1982, his eightieth birthday, Dad entered the grocery store as usual. He announced to the checkout woman, "I understand this store is giving gifts to anyone having an eightieth birthday." Without batting an eye, the woman responded, "Yes, we are!" Stepping around the counter, she stood on tiptoe and planted a kiss on Dad's cheek. Dad loved the attention.

It took several weeks before Dad shared this story with anyone. He says he didn't know how Mom would take it! We children told him to go ahead and tell her. When he finally got up enough courage and told her, she enjoyed the story too!

Dad was almost blindsided by people who wanted to show him kindness. As he approached the entrance to a public building, somebody would step up to hold the door. When his old Mercury sputtered and died, the next driver coming down the road would stop and offer help. When he had to go to church without Mom, family friends Joyce and her husband moved to sit close to him so that he was not alone in the pew.

Getting old has its own rewards. My dad learned to take full advantage of all the kindnesses offered him. One time Dad wanted to visit old friends, Kenneth and Rowena, at the convalescent home in nearby Hampton, Virginia.

He was in strange territory and couldn't read the street signs. Dad knew he kept making the wrong turns, and he was not getting any closer to his destination. Swallowing his pride, he asked for directions at two different gas stations. A sympathetic stranger said, "I'm going that way. Just follow me." Dad did.

All my life, I've had Dad as my model. Now that I am well into my seventies and he is no longer living, he is still a model. I recall fondly his sense of humor, his appreciation for others, his attitude that all strangers are potential friends. These are things I remember and love about my dad.

23

All Aboard the "Pass Christian Victory"

The heifers kicked and bawled and couldn't believe what was happening to them.

The year was 1949. Cattle boats were leaving my hometown of Newport News, Virginia, carrying farm animals to countries in war-torn Europe. Mennonite and Brethren men came from all over the United States to work on these boats.

The Brethren church had initiated a program of sending cattle and horses to war-torn places, in hopes of helping these countries to rebuild after the devastation of World War II. Mennonites joined the effort.

I was eighteen, recently graduated from high school, and eager for adventure. What an opportunity! I could see the world and at the same time make a contribution to the needs of a devastated country. With our parents' permission, and the blessing of the church, several of my friends joined me in signing up—Lewis Burkholder and Chris Yoder from my own community, along with Harold Buckwalter and Homer Wenger from Chesapeake.

This particular ship, the *Pass Christian Victory*, would take 850 heifers to the newly formed state of Israel. The ship was scheduled to sail in mid-November. We were instructed to be on call, prepared to leave when summoned. Each day I would go to the docks and watch the heifers being loaded, one by one, their crates lifted by crane and pulley from the dock onto the ship.

The date of departure had to be postponed several times when technical problems developed. Fear and excitement and anticipation built while we waited for the call that all was ready. Finally on November 16 we were summoned to report for duty. The ship would leave at 6:00 p.m. that same day.

My parents and sister and girlfriend came to the dock to say farewell. The whistle blew and the ship set sail. I recall waving good-bye and then standing at the rails and watching the lights recede along the shore. I remember the gentle swell of the Chesapeake Bay as we left the docks.

I had heard stories about seasickness. I felt fortunate that, in all my years of fishing on the Warwick and James rivers, I had never experienced this problem. I went to my bunk that night enjoying the smooth roll of the ship. I slept soundly.

In the morning, still feeling rather smug about my good health and eager to face my first day at sea, I stretched one foot out of bed, touched the floor, and realized I had to run quickly to reach the rail. I was sick. Very, very sick.

The next days were sheer agony. All I can remember is how sick I was. My friends tell me that I lay in the aisles and they had to step over me, while I groaned and moaned and hoped to die. They quote me as saying, "I just want to see my girlfriend one more time and then I want to die."

The seas grew even more turbulent. Huge waves splashed onto deck. Occasionally a big fish would wash aboard. Some heifers that could not take the rough seas died and had to be hoisted overboard. They were drawn into the powerful wake of the ship and could be seen for miles. It was an awful sight.

More than a hundred of the animals died and were buried at sea.

On the third day, my stomach settled down. I climbed out of the bunk and joined the workforce. Most of my friends had signed up as cattlemen, or cowboys, who would take care of the young Holstein heifers, feeding them and keeping them comfortable on the long voyage.

We were asked if we wanted to sign on as milkers and earn an extra $25. I was used to milking Daisy, our little Jersey cow at home who gave two quarts of milk morning and evening. So why not sign up as a milker? The $25 was a welcome bonus. Several of us signed up for the extra work.

What a disastrous decision that turned out to be! When we hit rough seas these young heifers started dropping their calves, calves that weren't supposed to be born until the ship arrived at its destination. When we tried to corner these feisty heifers for milking, they were not amused. They would look at me as if to say, "Now what are you planning to do?" They kicked, they bawled, they couldn't believe what was happening to them.

When I tell this story, I am asked why the calves couldn't be with their mothers and we would not have had to milk these restless animals. I don't know the answer to that. I just know the calves were kept separate from their mothers.

We gave some of the milk to the calves, and the excess milk was thrown overboard. And there was a lot of excess. These cows were giving at least three gallons each milking!

We learned to put clamps on their legs and tie them tight in a corner to separate the one cow from the other twenty-five sharing the stall. Milking was laborious, scary, and dangerous.

More and more calves were born. Finally I was milking twenty-five cows a day. We started milking at 5:00 a.m. and milked all morning until 11:00. Right after lunch we started in again, and milked until 7:00 p.m.

My hands ached. I was numb from all this milking. During that whole trip, I wrote only two letters to my girlfriend, and two to my family. The letters were hard to read and described the difficult life of a professional milker.

What a welcome sight when we passed the Rock of Gibraltar and knew that we were nearing our destination. Soon the Holstein cows would be in the hands of their new owners and my own hands would get back to normal.

NOTE: Heifer Project International was the outgrowth of one man's vision. Dan West, lifelong Brethren and conscientious objector during World War I, dreamed of bringing cows to impoverished countries. The idea was to give each family a cow, with the stipulation that its offspring must be given to another family and so on. I believe the first shipment of heifers went to Puerto Rico in 1944. The Heifer Project lives on. Their Christmas catalogue is my favorite of all catalogues.

24

"Cowboys" Touring the Holy Lands

*All through the sightseeing
we had to take care of the drunken sailors.*

For two weeks we navigated the Atlantic Ocean with twenty-five Mennonite/Brethren men and about thirty-five merchant marines.

What a contrast between the groups. The merchant marines were tough sailors who occupied their time playing cards for money, smoking, talking rough, trying to (and succeeding in) shocking us with their worldly ways. Each man on board had a daily allotment of one pack of cigarettes, and the sailors hounded the nonsmoking cowboys for the extra packs.

These two weeks seemed like a long, long time. In the middle of the Atlantic, no land in sight, no other ships on the horizon, ours was a very small vessel in a vast ocean. We watched eagerly for any glimpse of land, any sign of life.

On the tenth day the coast of Spain came into view, then the Rock of Gibraltar. We passed through the Straits of Gibraltar and watched the mountainous landscape of North Africa. We entered the Mediterranean Sea and finally reached our destination, Haifa, Israel.

When the boat docked at the port of Haifa, Israeli dignitaries were there to welcome us. On the pier a band played as we straggled down the gangplank, trying to get our land legs. It was a grand celebration! We learned that we were to be official guests of the Israeli government.

We were treated like royalty. For the next six days we toured the ancient and revered places of the Holy Land. The government provided two large buses and guides. We stayed in comfortable hotels and ate delicious food.

The contrast between the merchant marines and the Mennonite and Brethren cowboys became even more evident. The tough sailors looked forward to shore leave with two things in mind: wine and women. They immediately found their alcohol, and from then on, for the rest of the visit, they had to be helped on and off the bus as we tried to follow our tour leaders.

All through the Holy Land, the cowboys had to look out for the drunken sailors. Visit the village of Nazareth and hold up the inebriated man stumbling beside you. Walk through the Garden of Gethsemane, and turn to support the confused sailor. Drive to the Sea of Galilee, and help a man off the bus. And all the time, listen to the men calling for the bus to "Stop! Stop!" so they could find a restroom. What a spectacle we must have been!

Evenings we were on our own. We spent time in the city of Jerusalem looking through the markets for suitable gifts to take back to family and girlfriends. Betty still has the hand-embroidered blue scarf I found for her there.

Then it was time to board the ship and head for home. Whistles blew as we steamed out of Haifa. Time to rest? No! Now it was time to clean the ship. We tossed manure overboard. We raked the holds clean. Then we mopped and scrubbed and scrubbed some more. By the time we powered into Newport News, Virginia, we had a gleaming ship, ready to be inspected by U.S. government officials.

We arrived home one week before Christmas. The ship left the very next week with another load of cattle.

As I write these pages, I have contacted several of the other cowboys. It is a pleasure to remember such a significant happening. It was an important adventure, opening our eyes to the needs of the world. And most of all, as young Christians we were part of a huge effort helping to provide assistance to countries in need.

25

Greystone Park

*We all tried to stay
alert to any approaching bishops.*

I was twenty-two years old and I had huge decisions to make. My draft classification was I-W which meant that I could be called into service at any time. I knew I could never join the war effort. For my whole life I had been taught that war is wrong, that we should love our enemies and be willing to work for the benefit of mankind. It never entered my head to join the military. I would need to find another way to serve my country.

As long as I stayed in school I could be deferred. But school no longer was an option. I had finished one year of classes at Eastern Mennonite College and decided that I was not "college material." I simply could not concentrate. I liked working with my hands. I liked building things, but I did not like to sit at a desk reading and writing.

Betty and I had been married for two years and were both full-time college students. Betty enjoyed classes but agreed with me that we should go ahead and fulfill my draft requirements. We started making phone calls and looking for approved institutions where I could do alternate service, or I-W as it is called.

We received a list of places that were hiring conscientious objectors (COs) and contacted several of them. We heard from

Greystone Park near Morristown, New Jersey, and were invited to apply. We received authorization from the draft board and drove to New Jersey for a job interview.

The hospital was a huge institution with spacious grounds and impressive buildings. This description on Wikipedia matches my present memory of Greystone Park in the 1950s:

> A self-contained community that included staff housing, a post office, fire and police stations, a working farm, recreational facilities. It had its own gas and water utilities and a *gneiss* quarry, which was the source of the Greystone building material.... The Greystone grounds with rolling greens, lavish gardens, and fountain features were designed to aid in the treatment of the mentally ill.

Because I was a married man, Betty and I would not be eligible for housing on the grounds. We rented the upstairs apartment of a house on a quiet street in Morristown. We furnished the apartment with the truckload of furniture brought from our tiny apartment near Eastern Mennonite College at Harrisonburg, Virginia.

We were definitely out of our comfort zone. We had thought the college community was very different from our life in the Mennonite Colony of Newport News, but in New Jersey we found a setting that was really different. Apparently other young couples from Mennonite and Brethren communities also felt out of place. We shared each other's stories and laughed at our innocence.

For instance, on my first day on the job, my new boss, Gus, introduced me to other farm workers. All at once, somebody started to laugh, and I laughed too. I didn't know what was so funny, but it seemed appropriate to join in the laughter. It took me awhile to realize that the farm crew was made up of hired workers and mental health patients. The laughter was coming from a patient and myself. I stopped laughing.

Harold and Ruthie came to Greystone Park not long after we arrived. They, too, needed to find their own living quarters.

Harold answered an ad and stood on the front porch in a nice neighborhood to inquire about the availability of the apartment. He explained to the lady of the house that he was a CO and she replied, "Oh, a commanding officer!" She rented the apartment to him. It was the nicest of any in our circles.

Another story we laughed at involved "Goody," a Mennonite who was trying to distance himself from his home community. Goody was working on the Greystone farm one day when a Lancaster bishop came to visit him and greeted him with the holy kiss. Talk about embarrassment!

Goody's bishop, in his plain garb, looked like a Catholic priest, but priests didn't observe this biblical teaching (see 1 Peter 5:14). After that we all watched for approaching bishops.

We had to learn to adjust to the ways of the north. Or, more exactly, to the rhythm of work at an institution. One day the farm boss, Gus, directed me to one of the farm buildings and told me to clean the place. In about two hours I had the job done and reported back to Gus. I could tell that he didn't want to see me. I had finished the job too soon. I had to learn to slow down to the pace of the institution.

In New Jersey we used some weekends to see life in the big city. We often drove to New York City, about an hour away. We went to basketball games at Madison Square Garden. One year we watched the lighting of the Christmas tree at Rockefeller Center. We heard famous speakers at Youth for Christ meetings. We watched Herb Shriner produce his weekly TV talk show and remember the Chesterfield commercials when cigarette boxes with great-looking legs danced across the stage.

During the summer months we traveled the New Jersey Turnpike and were delayed in long lines of vacationers trying to exit at Asbury Park. We learned that in New Jersey you had to pay to swim in the Atlantic Ocean.

I was glad when my term of service was finished. We rented a U-Haul and moved our stuff back to Denbigh, Virginia, to set up housekeeping once again in the Colony.

26

An Unexpected Friend and Mentor

The small man dressed in black looked like a holy man.

My two years in I-W service (1954-1956) near Morristown, New Jersey, seem like a distant memory. It was not the most settled period of my life. My choices were to stay in school or respond to the military draft. School was not going well, and as a conscientious objector to war I needed to find employment in federally approved "Alternate Service" (I-W).

Greystone Park, also known as New Jersey State Hospital, was a mental health facility built in the 1800s, on seven hundred acres of land, near Morristown, N.J. I learned that the facility was home to 7,500 patients and more than 2,000 employees.

Probably thirty I-W men were already working at Greystone Park. They were employed as hospital aides, painters, carpenters, dairy workers, farm helpers, and mechanics.

I was hired as a farm helper and joined a crew of twelve or fourteen men. Two other conscientious objectors worked on the farm. Our boss was a man named Gus. Gus and his crew were responsible for the field crops and vegetable garden.

I was far from home. New Jersey seemed like foreign (and sometimes unfriendly) territory. But I settled into my new job and decided to make it a positive experience.

One day I was feeding corn into the silo and became aware that someone was standing nearby watching. I turned and saw a small man dressed in black from head to toe. He looked like a holy man. Maybe I was being visited by a Catholic priest? There were a lot of priests in New Jersey.

As he smiled and reached out his hand, I realized my visitor was John (J. C.) Wenger from Goshen, Indiana. What on earth was J. C. doing this far from home? I had not seen him for years, maybe not since he was a visitor in my parents' home.

J. C. explained that he just wanted to look me up and see how my life was going. We had a brief conversation there in the barn and then he left.

What a huge affirmation. It is a highlight of my memories from Greystone Park. I wonder how far J. C. traveled to visit one isolated young man. I must have corresponded with him after that visit because recently I found a letter written by J. C. in 1962. He writes, "Dear Brother in the Faith, Your letter of last summer reporting your plans to enter EMC [Eastern Mennonite College] this fall was a source of real encouragement to me."

Brother, friend, mentor. When I read now about J. C. Wenger in the *Mennonite Encyclopedia* I realize what a big man he was, how much he cared about the church, how influential he was in the church and beyond.

And he cared about me. J. C. was and is a huge inspiration to me even though he is no longer living.

27

The Best Storyteller of All

The man's young son sat nearby intently watching his father's face.

Our family has always enjoyed camp settings. When Betty and I are asked to lead retreats at a camp, we accept as often as possible. We have great memories of family weeks and pastors' retreats and marriage enrichment weekends.

Camps we have especially enjoyed are Laurelville Mennonite Church Center in western Pennsylvania, Spruce Lake in the Poconos, and Highland Retreat in western Virginia, as well as Brethren Woods in the Shenandoah Valley of Virginia.

We need the change of pace away from church and school schedules, and we need the change of scenery when we can focus on the beauties of mountains and lakes and trees. We enjoy the swimming pools, guided hikes, games, and activities planned by camp leaders. We like meeting people from distant places. It is a time of renewal and relaxation.

Have you noticed how the interaction of a group changes depending on the surroundings? In a formal setting, we tend to maintain a rather proper appearance and formal communication. A camp setting invites a different kind of connection.

Somehow it is easier to let down the barriers and be a little more disclosing with each other.

By the end of family week, for example, when families were learning to know each other, we would plan an evening of storytelling. For this particular evening, families would not be separated. Fathers and mothers and children stayed together for this special time of telling stories.

I especially remember one such evening. One of the fathers attending family week had a noticeable speech impediment. All week, as we approached the evening of storytelling, I was concerned that he might not feel able to participate. So far, he had taken an active part in the week's activities but he seldom spoke. He sat beside his wife and she did the talking.

This particular evening I remember as almost miraculous. This man started to tell a story. By now he knew the group and they knew him. In this accepting, affirming, appreciative group he opened up.

His young son sat nearby intently watching his father's face. At first, the son seemed tense and self-conscious. Then he saw the other listeners become relaxed and responsive. By the end of the story, his face was one big smile. His dad was the best storyteller of all!

28

Seminarians in Training

We had a mock funeral with an empty casket.

After graduating from Eastern Mennonite College at Harrisonburg, Virginia, I looked forward to attending Union Theological Seminary (UTS), a Presbyterian institution in Richmond, Virginia. It would be a welcome change from the Mennonite schools I had attended for seven years.

At UTS we first-year students were dubbed juniors. Second year students were middlers and seniors were called seniors. It was gratifying to not be labeled as freshmen, but indeed we were a class of green, inexperienced students.

The seminary had a 150-year history. Its stated mission was to provide "education for Christian ministry that is scholarly, pastoral, and engaged with contemporary life."

Through its long history, the faculty at UTS must have learned that these future pastors would need a lot of help getting ready to lead a congregation. And they were determined to send out preachers who were acquainted with the wounded and hurting at our doorstep. We would have to remove our rose-tinted glasses and see society through new lenses.

City officials and church leaders came to address the student body. I remember that Eleanor Parker Sheppard, the first woman mayor of Richmond, spoke to us. She recalled that when she was a child her family would drive into the city, and how she dreaded the trip through areas of slums and poverty and scenes of crime.

By 1964 the bypass kept the main traffic out of those sections. One could get to center city without being aware of the poverty and crime. You didn't have to witness the pain. Mrs. Sheppard wanted us to be aware of those areas and the people living there, and not forget their presence in the city.

We had class members who had never been to a funeral, so our professors, with the help of a funeral director, planned a day of funeral activities. We visited a funeral home. We had a mock funeral with an empty casket. We followed the hearse to a cemetery and had a burial service.

Most of us had never visited a psychiatric hospital. The class traveled to Williamsburg, Virginia, to spend a day at Eastern State Hospital. We individually visited the various wards and spent time with patients and staff members. We learned that these were real people in need of individual attention.

By the time I enrolled at UTS I was already thirty-five years old with a wife and two young children. Betty and I thought it made good sense to buy a house in Richmond, but that meant selling our new home in Harrisonburg. (If we had known that we would be in Richmond only one year, we would never have sold the little house in the Valley. We would have found tenants and would ourselves have been renters in Richmond.)

Near the end of my first year at Union, I received the call to return to Eastern Mennonite College to become campus pastor. This appealed to me. I considered this the chance of a lifetime.

So we reluctantly left the seminary in Richmond and moved back to the Valley.

29

Our New Neighbor, Cousin Ivy

She stood on a plank at the front door and said, "Just put me to work."

We moved back to Harrisonburg, Virginia ("the Valley") after one year of living in Richmond and attending Union Theological Seminary. Before we moved, we made several trips to the Valley looking for rental property. We found a nice, older house on quiet Shenandoah Street just a few blocks from Eastern Mennonite College where I would be employed.

We walked the length of the street and noticed an elderly woman in her garden. She stopped working to introduce herself. She said, "You can call me Cousin Ivy and I really am your cousin." She explained how we were related. It was complicated, but I took her word for it. We could tell she would be a friend in our new neighborhood.

A few weeks later, the huge Allied Van drove up Shenandoah Street with all our earthly belongings. We stood in our new living room watching the activity. Three burly men emerged from the truck and laid down the planks to form a bridge from the truck to our front door.

Before the men could get the first piece of furniture off the truck, here came Cousin Ivy down the street. She came onto the porch, stepped onto a plank, and stood at the front door saying, "I'm here to help. You just put me to work."

What a sight! Our new-old, friendly cousin, wanting to be a good neighbor, stood right in the middle of everything, blocking the way of the movers. As gently as possible we invited her into the living room, off to the side so the men could get on with their work.

We learned to know Cousin Ivy well and appreciated her sense of humor. One day as I walked by her house she was setting out tomato plants. I complimented her on her garden and said, "Cousin Ivy, you are getting an early start with your tomato plants." She laughed and said, "The problem is, I'm jerking them out faster than I'm putting them in." But she was not letting her palsy get the best of her.

Cousin Ivy was a delightful neighbor. She was loved and respected in her community. I'm glad we were able to live for a time in her neighborhood and enjoy this kind of friendship with a distant cousin.

30

The Gift of Grace
(*Sermon*)

*That night Parker dreamed
that he was held in the arms of God.*

Scripture: Acts 9:17-28

The Bible is full of stories of spiritual friendships, stories of one person giving grace to another. Acts 9 records such a story.

Saul had been mean and hostile to the early church.
　*He was a tormentor and a menace to
the people of the New Way.*
　*Then on the road to Damascus he was
struck down by a light from heaven.*
*"He fell to the ground and heard a voice say,
'Saul, Saul, why do you persecute me?'*
　*For three days he was blind,
　　and did not eat or drink anything."*
He asks, "Who are you, Lord?"
He hears the voice of God
　and he is transformed.

He becomes the chief advocate of the New Way.

 But the Christians still remember him as a terrorist.
They don't believe he can change.
He has caused such severe persecution.
He was such a mean person.

 Back in Damascus,
  Ananias is called by God to
  go to Saul.
At first Ananias refuses.
 He is afraid of Saul.
He has heard all the stories about this man
 and all the harm he has done to Christians.
But God says,
"Go! This man is my chosen instrument
  to carry my name to the Gentiles and their kings
   and to the people of Israel.
Baptize him
and bring to him the gift of the Holy Spirit."
Ananias went, and
Saul was restored.

Ananias was a giver of grace
 and became a spiritual friend to Saul.

Later in chapter 9 we see more of the same thing with other believers. Saul is preaching and declaring the good news. He tries to join the disciples in Jerusalem. But they hold him at arms' length. They are afraid of Saul. Why should they put themselves in harm's way?

This time Barnabas steps forward
 and tells the story of Saul's conversion.
The disciples are convinced,
 and they receive Saul with open arms.

Barnabas gives the gift of grace

and becomes Saul's spiritual friend.
"Then the church
   throughout Judea, Galilee and Samaria
enjoyed a time of peace.
   It was strengthened;
and encouraged by the Holy Spirit,
   it grew in numbers,
living in the fear of the Lord." v. 31

Many people were added to the church during this period.

We are called to be like Ananias and Barnabas. We are called to give grace to others. I am called to become a spiritual friend. Consider this story that Parker Powell tells in his book, *Let Your Life Speak*:

Parker was experiencing major depression.
   He describes it as a time when he was snakebit.
He was numb. He could feel nothing.
   Life was a burden and a pain.
He hated to get up in the morning
   and he hated every hour of the day.
He would rather be dead!

During this dreadful time,
   his friends came to cheer him
and sought to bring healing and hope.
   They tried every way they knew
to lift his spirits,
   but nothing helped.

Some friends said,
   "Come on Parker, let's go outside
      and enjoy this beautiful day.
Let's look at the flowers
   and the sunshine and the beautiful earth.
If you come outside,
   surely your spirits will be lifted."

But nothing changed. Everything was dark

and in shadows.
Parker could feel nothing.

Other friends said, "Parker, you have
    written so many books,
        and have helped countless people,
            how can you feel so depressed and sad?"
But Parker could not remember his good works.
    He felt worthless.

Others said,
"We know exactly how you feel;
    We have been there, too."
And Parker knew that no one ever knows
    exactly how you feel.
He continued to feel hopeless.

Then one day a man came,
    a man without many words,
and he just sat with Parker.
    They sat in silence.
Finally the man spoke and said,
    "Parker, may I remove your shoes and massage your feet?"
Parker agreed.

While the friend massaged his feet,
    Parker realized
    that his feet were the only *part of him that had any life left.*

That night Parker dreamed that he was
    held in the arms of God
and God was saying,
    "Parker, you are my beloved child
        and I am well pleased."

In the morning,
    the depression had lifted
And Parker felt life and hope returning.

    That story holds some valuable clues as to how we might be givers of God's grace and become spiritual friends to each other.

1. Listening

We are at our best when we slow down
    enough to listen.
Sometimes the pain is too deep for words.
    Words cannot fix the pain.
Being there and listening is all we can do.
Through listening
    we can show compassion and mercy.
Sometimes we need to wait in silence
    for God to come and bring healing.
Through listening I might become a spiritual friend
    and be a giver of grace.

2. Going

Some of us go to the places where no one else is going,
    and there we become the hands and feet of Jesus.
Tony Campola tells this story:

One day on the streets of Philadelphia
    a street person approached Tony.
The man was dirty and needed a bath.
    His beard was matted with yesterday's food.
The man was drinking a cup of McDonald's coffee
    and held out the cup, offering Tony a sip of coffee.
Tony's first impulse was to reject the man,
    to say no
    and head on down the street as fast as possible.

But something held him back.
    He explains,
"All of a sudden I saw in the man the image of Jesus.
    I took the coffee and drank from the cup.
The man thanked me profusely,
    and I felt the presence of Jesus."

Can we go to the places where there is no presence
    and there be the hands and feet of Jesus?

3. Hope-Giving

Many people that we meet
*   feel hopeless,*
*   torn by a meaningless existence.*
They don't know what the day will bring forth.
*   They ask, "Where is God in all this wreckage?"*
They feel depressed and snakebit.

Can I be available to bring healing?
*   Can I become a spiritual friend?*
*   Can I wash the feet of a stranger?*

Is there a way we can take our present friendships
*   and develop a way of speaking to one another*
*   that would build one another up*
*   in our spiritual life?*

It would be difficult but not impossible
*   to call a friend and say,*
"I need to have a spiritual conversation with somebody.
*   Would you be willing to be a listener?"*

And we could come prepared with questions
*   that would keep us on track.*

Here are some questions that I found in a book
*   by Wendy Miller, called* Learning to Listen: A Guide for Spiritual Friends:

*   1. How has God been at work in my life this week?*
*   2. What have been the signs of God's grace to me?*
*   3. What may have blocked God's grace to me?*
*   4. How have I been "in the stream of God's grace" this week?*
*   5. What sins do I have to confess?*

These questions are one way to be accountable to each other.
We can use the questions as a guide
*   when we feel our faith is weak,*
*   when we face perplexing questions*
*   and have decisions to make,*
*   when changes are called for.*

I ask myself,
   Can I be attentive to my spiritual friend?
   Can I listen in love,
      compassionately,
         reflectively?

Can I allow my friend to do the same for me?

If so, we can become grace-givers for each other.
   We can build a spiritual friendship.
      We can help each other on the journey.

Amen.

31

The Gift of Sight

"Mom! The boy has lost his eye."

Recently when I kept my regular appointment with Dr. Paul Yoder, he reported that my eyesight had not changed at all in the last three years.

What a gift! How thankful I am for good eyesight. The recent minor irritations (like having to replace my glasses after they were crushed under the lawn mower) really are minor.

At such times I remember how close I came to losing sight in one eye. What a scary time that was. And how scary it was for my parents.

Dad was taking me for a ride through the orchard. He had hitched the horse to the farm wagon and we were inspecting the long row of apple trees. The harness snagged a tree branch, and when the horse jerked loose, the limb swung sharply across the wagon. It caught me squarely in the face. The gnarly branch raked across my eye and scrambled it into a bloody mess.

Dad hoisted me into his arms and headed for the house. I still remember the desperation in his voice as he cried out, "Mom! The boy has lost his eye."

(In such an emergency, Dad was not able to keep his cool, especially when his children were in trouble. What I remember most about that awful day are those terrified words of Dad.)

Visiting in our home that week was John R. Mumaw, in the community for revival meetings. Brother Mumaw joined the frightened circle. He cradled my face in his hands and prayed for healing. Then all of us headed downtown to the doctor's office.

The doctor did emergency surgery and wrapped my face in a huge bandage. We were supposed to come back in two weeks to find out if I still had sight in that eye. For two weeks I was the object of prayer and careful attention. Everybody treated me like a celebrity. They pitied me and were afraid that I would be blind in that eye for life.

When the two weeks were up, Mom and Dad and I headed back to the doctor. My parents tell me they could not bear to look when the bandage was removed. Instead, they watched the face of the doctor. When he smiled, they knew the answer. Their tears turned to smiles. I could see!

The work of a faithful doctor, the prayers of the visiting evangelist, and the wonderful healing that God brings in restoring health to our physical bodies—these were my thoughts when I heard Dr. Yoder say, "Your eyes haven't changed at all in the last three years!"

32

Meeting at Harper's Ferry

We retraced the steps of our ancestor and met a famous person of our own era.

I wanted to escape. Was I trying to avoid turning seventy, or did I just need to get away from home while it happened? Whatever the case, I started making plans to leave the house for a couple of days and celebrate this new milestone among strangers.

Harper's Ferry in West Virginia had been on our list of places to visit. This was the site where Great-Grandmother Susanna Heatwole Brunk made her famous crossing of the Potomac River.

The brave young woman was riding to meet her husband, Henry, in Hagerstown, Maryland. Henry was a conscientious objector to war. He had escaped the military headhunters in the Shenandoah Valley and had sent word to his wife to join him in Hagerstown. But when she arrived at the Harper's Ferry crossing, the bridge was on fire.

This seemed the right time for us to explore Harper's Ferry, to stand at the historic spot and read again about the courageous ride. MapQuest showed us that driving to Harper's Ferry from our home at Harrisonburg, Virginia, would be easy. It would take about two hours on roads through scenic countryside.

So on the morning of May 19, 2001, Betty and I set out on this adventure. We drove north on Interstate 81, through New Market, then turned east toward Charlestown and Berryville. In no time we were following US-340 North, crossing into West Virginia. Soon we saw the signs directing us to Harpers Ferry National Park. The day was gorgeous and the scenery so beautiful we wondered why we had not made this special trip before.

We parked in the designated area and made our way toward the river. We walked around for awhile, getting a feel of the place, trying to decide just where Great-Grandmother might have forded the river. We walked out on one of the bridges that cross the river. Betty said to me, "You stand right here and I will read you the story."

About that time, a group of tourists came by, following a park ranger across the bridge. The park ranger must have heard snatches of the story and she asked, "What is the little book? Is it history from this place?" And I replied, "It's a story of my great-grandmother during the Civil War when she tried to cross the Potomac and the bridge was burning and she had to ride her horse across."

We asked the ranger if she knew where the original bridge was located. Her reply was another history lesson. Because of its strategic location, she explained, both the Union and Confederate troops moved through Harper's Ferry. The town changed hands eight times between 1861 and 1865 and the bridge was set on fire at least eight times.

The ranger said, "We would love to have a copy of the booklet. When I finish leading this walking tour, I could take the book to the office and have it copied."

A member of the group stepped forward and said to the ranger, "Please go ahead. We can take care of ourselves while you go to the office." We glanced at the man who was making this offer. He looked familiar. Betty tried to nudge me. She wanted to signal me that we were meeting an important person. She tried again, and finally she said to the man, "We know you, don't we?"

He was such a gentleman. He acknowledged that he was Clarence Thomas, the most recent justice appointed to the United States Supreme Court. He wanted to introduce all the members of his party. He wanted to know our names and all about our historic great-grandmother.

We had a delightful conversation with the eight or ten persons with Judge Thomas who were on a day trip from Washington, D.C. When the ranger came back, we said good-bye to the group and headed back the way we had come.

We remembered the long days and weeks of watching the confirmation hearings. One day we believed Anita Hill, the woman who accused Thomas of sexual harassment, and the next day we were convinced that Thomas was the one telling the truth.

What an historic day! Not only had we retraced the steps of our ancestor, but we had met a famous person of our own era. We walked in silence for awhile. Then one of us said, "Clarence Thomas. We don't even like him." And the other replied, "We do now!"

Part 2
DO JUSTICE, LOVE KINDNESS

Introduction

Somewhere I read that all personal theology should begin with the words, "Let me tell you a story." This is my belief. I hope that when you read these stories, you will be reminded of your own journey, and you will tell your stories, too.

Jesus is our model storyteller. Some of his most important teachings come to us through stories simple yet profound:
- the son who runs away from home and gets a huge party when he returns;
- the woman who loses a coin, sweeps the whole house, then celebrates with her neighbors when the coin is found;
- the sheep that is lost and hopeless and then welcomed by the shepherd who takes her back into the sheepfold;
- the story of the seeds that fall on good ground or rocky soil;
- and the rich young ruler who is told to sell everything that he has.

Another story tells of the widow who bangs on the door at midnight. Jesus advises her to keep on banging until she gets what she needs. In the stories, Jesus is there to welcome, redeem, celebrate.

Often when I am with other pastors, they mention a story from my first book, *That Amazing Junk-Man,* remember a story from their own experience, and want to share it with me. Sometimes they add, "I am writing a book, too!" And I assure them that I will buy their book—I am glad to hear their stories also.

I want to keep learning from my friends and from my reading. I don't need to learn everything firsthand. For instance, in chapter 7, "The Best Seats in the House," I wish I had been more knowledgeable about other churches and their efforts to move the congregation into the front seats. I wish I had not taken it personally, wondering why some folks were choosing to sit as far as possible from the preacher.

We need each other. My life has been enriched by the interaction with members of the congregation. Their joys have made my life more celebrative. Their sorrows have taught me to be more in tune to the emotional and spiritual growth of myself and others.

Sue Monk Kidd talks about the kind of availability that I applaud and that I have tried to practice. In her book, *Firstlight* (Guideposts Books, 2007), she writes

> When you sit with a crying woman, just sit with her. . . . Be fully present. . . . Do it without passing judgment on her, wanting to convert her. . . . Do it the way Mary sat at the feet of Jesus—with an undivided heart.

Relationships matter to me. In chapter 21, "Finding Myself in Hot Water," I ask, "Aren't we to be compassionate as our Father in heaven is compassionate?" I want to radiate gentleness, kindness, forgiveness, and understanding. This is the kind of minister I have tried to be.

1

Do Justice, Love Mercy (*Sermon*)

*The Gestapo were chasing
the half-frozen woman.*

*Several years ago we traveled through Switzerland and Germany,
    visiting the land of our forebearers.
One of the places on the tour was
    the concentration camp at Dachau
where thousands of Jews were killed.
    Dachau was a dismal place.
We were overwhelmed with the aura of
    death and torture and horror.*

>   *This was not the only concentration camp.
>   In other regions of Germany the same things had happened.*

*Six million Jews were killed.
    Also killed were homosexuals,
        Jehovah's Witnesses,
            and others who did not fit the Nazi mold.*

>   *In contrast to this awful inhumanity,
>   I have been reading again the book,
>   Lest Innocent Blood Be Shed, by Philip Hallie.*

Hallie tells the story of a little French Village,
  Le Chambon,
and how goodness happened there.

André Trocmé was a pastor in this little village.
  André and his wife, Magda Trocmé,
    set the tone for goodness.

One night while closing up the parsonage,
  Mrs. Trocmé heard a knock at her front door.
Snow and wind were pounding against the house.
  They were snowbound!
    But she heard the knock,
      and she called out,
  "Come on in!"

The door opened, and Mrs. Trocmé
  realized that a Jewish woman was standing there,
    half frozen, fearful,
      fleeing her persecutors.
The Gestapo were chasing the woman.

The rule of the land was that
  anybody harboring a refugee
    would be put to death.
The pastor's wife
  knew she had to help,
    so she called out,
"Naturally, come on in."'
  She gave sanctuary to this cold, frightened, lonely
  woman.

In the days that followed,
  hundreds of Jewish refugees found refuge
    in the little village.
The watchword of the entire community was
"Naturally, come on in."

After the war ended,
    and all the evil was revealed,
        the villagers of Le Chambon were honored
  for their brave acts of hospitality.
Hundreds of lives had been saved by the
  brave people of the village
    with their motto, "Naturally, come on in."

In sharp contrast to Dachau and all its evil and destruction,
Le Chambon was known as a place of goodness.

Like the people of Le Chambon,
  God welcomes everyone to come.
    God says to all, "Naturally, come on in."

2

A Lenten Road Map (*Sermon*)

*Suffering is everywhere.
Are we weeping too?*

Luke 13:31-35

We are all on a Lenten Journey,
  a forty-day journey
    leading up to Easter Sunday.
We've eaten our Fasnachts,
we've had the ashes applied to our foreheads.

Now is a time of Reflection,
  Repentance,
    Preparation.
And on Easter morning
  God wakes us up!

Not far from here is a Catholic priest
  who is extra busy during this season of Lent.
You might have read about him in the newspaper.
During Lent, he hears many confessions.
  People are looking within,
    confessing their sins.

The priest listens all day long
    and is personally deeply moved.
He realizes that he too is a sinner
    in need of forgiveness.
Toward evening he slips away and
    finds another priest
So that he can make his own confession
    and be absolved of sin.

This is the week Jesus journeys to Jerusalem.
    Ninety *times in the Gospel of Luke*
        Jesus refers to Jerusalem
(more than all the other Gospels combined).

    On this day
Jesus stands looking over the Holy City of Jerusalem.
    He sees the indifference of the people
        and their hardness of heart
        and he weeps.

    In deep sadness, Jesus says:
"O Jerusalem, Jerusalem,
    You who kill the prophets and stone those sent to you,
        how often I have longed to gather your children
            together,
as a hen gathers her chicks under her wings,
but you were not willing!" —*Luke 13:34*

Jerusalem is filled with hatred and violence.
    The people reject Jesus' offer of love and forgiveness.
Jesus weeps bitter tears.
    He is rejected and left alone.

There is passion and intensity in Jesus
    as he journeys to the cross.
Luke's narrative is sobering.
    Jesus faces many musts.

            He must *be on the way.*
            He must *go to Jerusalem.*

> *He* must *go to the temple.*
> *He* must *go to Gethsemane.*
> *He* must *go to Calvary and the cross.*
> *Nothing will stop him now.*
> *He is on the way.*

One of the books that has touched me deeply is *Exclusion and Embrace,* by Miroslav Volf. Volf stands and looks over Bosnia, his homeland, and he weeps. His own people have experienced ethnic cleansing, murder, and rape. Volf asks, "How can we live in a world like this?" He wonders, and agonizes, and finally says, "The only way is to forgive, even when it is impossible to forgive. Forgive and forget just as Jesus did."

Volf describes a God
whose very nature is to forgive,
> *who puts our sins behind his back,*
>> *and remembers them no more.*

He describes the movement of God in four distinct steps:
> *1. God waits for us with open arms.*
> *2. God is patient and refuses to give up on any of us.*
> *3. God closes his arms around us, embracing us as his children.*
> *4. God opens his arms and wants us to be free. (pp. 142-144)*

Jesus will give his life for Jerusalem.
> *He wants to replace violence and sadness*
> *with joy and happiness.*
He wants to give them his life.

Today we are invited to look within,
to seek an abundant life.
Today, when I read this story, I remember the words
> *in our old hymnal:*
> *"Come into my heart, Lord Jesus,*
> *there is room in my heart for you."*

Today I ask:
> *Is there a* must *in my life (as in Jesus' life)?*

Is there a burning compassion?
    When is the last time I have wept?

Look at the social needs of our own cities.
See the images of war and violence around the world.
    The wounded stare at us with haunted eyes.
        The dead lie in the streets in pools of blood.
            Smoke and flames rise out of bombed-out vehicles.
Suffering is everywhere.
Are we weeping too?

William Barclay, the preacher who wrote commentaries
    many years ago,
Observed that there are two important days in every life:
    1. The day you were born.
    2. The day you understood why.

Let us all get out our Lenten road maps
    finding places of repentance and renewal,
        finding ways to give ourselves in loving service
    in a world of pain and hurt.

   The journey is not just about Good Friday and Easter.
        It is about the places along the way.
        It is about doing the work of Easter.

Forgiven and embraced
    by a Holy God
we are commissioned to do his work in the world.
Let this be our Lenten journey.

Amen.

3

All That I Have

*Three dimes were
taped across the top of the letter.*

I found myself in the Hallmark shop, desperately looking for a card that would convey the desired message. I found one that seemed to fit my purpose. With tiny hearts all around the outer edge, the front of the card carried these words: "Don't think you are indispensable. . . ." then opened to the inside message, "Just because I can't get along without you."

This trip to town was giving me a much-needed break from my desk in the Office of Development of Eastern Mennonite College. It was time for another mass mailing, asking (begging) our friends and supporters once more to open their pockets and share their wealth.

It was my opinion that these mailings happened too often. But what should I do? How could a small church college function without generous friends who would keep us out of the red?

This was my first year working in the development office. Until that year I had filled the role of pastor of students, and it was my favorite job of all time. But this particular year, President Myron Augsburger had asked, then pleaded, then demanded, that I take on the "challenge" of this new position.

When he first asked, I had prayed, searched, weighed carefully, and declined his request.

President Augsburger was persuasive. He was himself trying to leave the country for a year in Europe. And even from the airport, he called with his urgent request. Finally, I saw no way to avoid the assignment.

My coworkers in the development office were dedicated, hard-working staff members. I enjoyed the daily interaction with them. They tried to teach me the joys of asking people for money. I was supposed to learn that WE were actually giving THEM a gift when we offered them the opportunity to make contributions to our worthy organization. Together we celebrated when our efforts paid off and gifts came in.

But here I was in the Hallmark store looking for some inspiration for yet another appeal. I smiled to myself as I bought the card. I could use the Valentine theme, hook them with this catchy phrase, then get serious about our financial needs.

The letter was mailed to our friends. In the coming weeks we received the anticipated responses. Some pretty significant gifts came in. One day as I was opening the mail, I found a letter with three dimes taped across the top. A little handwritten note said, "I have looked all over the house and this is all I can find. I hope God can use this in your ministry. God bless you."

Like the woman in the Bible, this woman had given all that she had. I kept the letter on the corner of my desk for a long time and thanked God for people like this widow who give life and hope and inspiration to those who work in the development office.

Indeed, as I think of the needs of our church institutions, and when I open one of the many appeals that come to our house, I often think of the little Valentine note: "Don't think you are indispensable. . . . Just because I can't get along without you!"

4

When Sam Calls, You Pay Attention

He can look you straight in the eye and tell you what he wants from you.

"Have you gone to your non-assertiveness training yet?"

Whenever I meet Sam around town, we both know this will be my first question.

A lot of people in my circles really should attend a good assertiveness training workshop. They are too mild-mannered and sweet and quiet. They can't express their thoughts or make their wishes known. Some could even be described as passive-aggressive in their desire to get their way and their inability to be forthright in their communication.

This is not Sam's problem. He can look you straight in the eye and tell you what he wants from you. Sometimes, seemingly without conscience, he asks for more than you want to give. And you have to be assertive enough to stand up to him.

Sam has worn many hats in his lifetime. I first knew him as a young boy in Virginia, when his parents moved from Pennsylvania to work with the sailors onboard the ships docked in Newport News. Sam must have been preteen at the time of his parents' move. But he soon established himself in the young people's group, and he set his cap for one of the prettiest girls and talked Sarah into marriage.

This must have been his early training in assertiveness. Since then Sam has worked in many jobs that called for this kind of strength. After graduating from Eastern Mennonite College, he became dean of men at the college. Next he was principal at Eastern Mennonite High School for a number of years.

Sam was executive secretary of Virginia Mennonite Conference and pastor at Lindale Mennonite Church and then overseer in the Northern District of Virginia Conference. More recently he has served in the development office at Eastern Mennonite University.

When we worked together as overseers, Sam was usually full of creative ideas. He could present his proposals in a positive, forceful way, and build a convincing case. Once in this setting, I expressed aloud my thoughts that "Sam needs a good dose of non-assertiveness training." Everybody laughed and Sam laughed too.

At the local bagel shop there is a booth labeled "Sam's Place." I understand the shop owner installed the label. This is where Sam meets and greets those he plans to solicit. The five-dollar breakfast he buys for you could lead to more than you expected.

I tell Sam that he is the only Mennonite I know who should learn non-assertiveness. But assertiveness has worked well for Sam, and the institutions where he serves have benefited from his personality and his gifts. In fact, because of Sam's letter and phone call this week, I am writing my semiannual check to Eastern Mennonite University.

5

Overhearing the Gospel

*I invited a young boy
to sit on a stool while I sat nearby.*

There are no shortcuts to a good sermon. Preaching is hard work; that's all there is to it. You have heard the line, "A hot sun and a slow mule drove many a person to the ministry." But to me the ministry is every bit as hard and as hot as any of my previous work, whether in the peach orchard, on the carpentry crew, or in the fields at New Jersey State Hospital.

Reading about two books a week, building up a library, listening to countless tapes—these have helped me in the work of ministry. Fred Craddock is one such teacher and helper. In his book, *Overhearing the Gospel* (Abingdon Press), Craddock portrays Jesus directing his message to his disciples. Beyond this intimate circle, he says, "the crowds overheard the message."

An example in our own worship services is the children's story that captures the attention of the whole congregation. One Sunday morning I decided to follow this script for the morning for the "children's sermon."

I invited a young boy to sit on a stool while I sat nearby and told him the story of the prodigal son. I could relax and speak in a conversational tone. I was aware that those overhearing were unusually attentive that morning!

I learned (even if I had known it before) that—
- Sermons ought to be as simple and as easy to understand as a children's story.
- Indirect communication comes to the hearer at a slant which catches the hearer by surprise.
- Two things happen in overhearing—distance and participation. In distance, we are not assaulted. In participation, we feel drawn into the story.
- This method (overhearing the story) maximizes involvement in the story. We *become* prodigal sons and daughters on the journey back home to God.

That morning, in a simple message overheard, the listeners were invited to "come home to Jesus who waits with open arms."

6

Preacher's Kids

*Would Billy Graham
be able to help our son forgive?*

When I think of the label Preacher's Kid (PK), I think of the son or daughter who resents the role of the preacher/parent and who goes out of his or her way to become a humiliation to the family. In this story, the picture is turned the other way around. As I look back, I believe that my situation became an embarrassment and humiliation to our children, especially to our son.

Both Don and Kathleen have been cheerleaders and encouragers throughout my ministry. They have made countless sacrifices because of my pastoral role. For example, a day at the beach could be marked on the calendar for weeks and then at the last minute I would be needed for a funeral. The children were usually good sports about such a change of plans.

Coming back to our home church in Virginia as pastor was a bit scary. Lots of extended family members and old school friends were here. We knew it could put a strain on these relationships, but by this time we had been a pastor family for twenty years and thought we could survive any tension.

But things were not working out. Friends who tried to be helpful would say, "Please accept us as we are. Don't expect us to change." I spent sleepless nights not able to figure out what was wrong but knowing that things were not going well. Finally, we decided that for our own health and the health of the congregation, it was time to move on.

What a hard decision it was! We were embarrassed to admit defeat. We were ashamed to tell our families. Our daughter lived in another state, but our son lived in the area and had good friends in the church. He enjoyed working with the young people in the church. I believe he kept hoping for a miracle so that we would decide to stay.

Finally, we all agreed it was time to go. The day came for the moving van. Our small group came to help load the last of our belongings on the truck and they vacuumed each room as it emptied. Our beautiful home looked deserted. It was evening when we hugged our close friends and pulled away. Betty and I each drove a vehicle. We both admitted later that we cried for the first hour as we tried to focus on the highway.

Don remained in the area, and it would be weeks before I learned how he was processing our leaving. He wrote to Billy Graham! My son, the Preacher's Kid, was writing to the Billy Graham Evangelistic Association? Yes, he wrote how painful the past year had been. Would Billy Graham be able to help Don find some way to forgive the congregation and his parents for all this pain?

The response came in the form of a package. A little book fell into his lap—*Seventy Times Seven* by David Augsburger. David, our friend and cousin. What a surprise to have Dave ministering to our family by way of the Billy Graham Association!

7

The Best Seats in the House

I was tired of preaching to rows and rows of empty pews.

I watched the basket pass from hand to hand. It moved slowly from the side aisle to the center, then slipped to the next row before it continued its journey. As it made its way past the worshipers, some would smile and hand it to the next person. Others would hold it in their hands, study the contents, and help themselves before passing it along.

What was going on here? It was not yet time to collect our tithes and offerings. The gathering hymns were being sung, and we were settling in for the hour-long service.

I was so tired of standing up to preach to the rows and rows of empty pews. A few eighty-year-olds sat in these front seats, but the families and young children and teenagers all hung in the back. It felt like I was launching hand grenades toward the back pews.

The worship planners created interactive and participatory services, and we tried to include all ages in the morning worship hour. But why did some insist on choosing the back seats every Sunday morning? It was a discouraging, frustrating situation. I had not experienced this in other churches where I had served.

The previous week, a little note in the bulletin had said, "During the morning service, candy will be provided to those in the front four rows." The basket was supposed to offer a solution to our dilemma, so this morning I was alert for any changes.

The teenagers were responding! My eighty-year-old Aunt Edna had approved my far-fetched idea. And here she was in one of the front rows, trying to show support for this unorthodox idea. I saw her trying to keep a straight face as she took a mint from the basket.

We kept the candy baskets going for three months. It was a little expensive. I bought the candy from my own personal funds, but it seemed a friendly gesture and it offered something for the young people. And it certainly improved my attitude on a Sunday morning.

After a three-month period, we stopped passing the candy baskets. The novelty had worn off and it had become a little distracting. The young people in the front rows started choosing seats a little further back. I was baffled.

During this time, I was invited to speak one Sunday morning at a large, beautiful church in another city. To be sure I had found the right place I arrived thirty minutes early and went inside to meet with the pastor. I noticed that the parking lot was already filling up.

I asked a greeter, "Why are all these people here at this hour?" He replied, "Oh, they are the oldest members of the church and they come early every week so they can have the back rows. If they get here late, the back seats will be taken!"

So other churches had the same problem that we had! I didn't have to take it personally. But this was small comfort, and it continued to worry me.

Some years later, now serving at a different church, I read *Worship as Pastoral Care*, by William H. Willimon. In an excellent chapter, "Worship: The Near and Far of It," he explains that resistance itself may be an act of worship. He refers to Moses and Jonah and Paul as persons who resisted.

What a thought! Why hadn't I figured this out for myself? Why hadn't I been more tuned in to the backseat huggers at the previous church? Were those in the back somehow showing more respect for holy space than those who marched to the front of the church? Or were they experiencing feelings of alienation, rejection, or guilt?

I would have been a more compassionate pastor if I had taken the time to explore these possibilities. It certainly would have made me more accepting and understanding of those who did not come to the front pews to eat my candy!

8

Jud Finds a Way

*To clean ourselves off,
we went swimming in a crystal
blue mountain stream.*

Jud and Pam were dating, and they were getting serious. Pam had been baptized and joined the church the same day her mother and stepfather came into church membership.

Jud was not ready to make this step. He needed to do more thinking. It might have been our church's position on war and killing. As Mennonites we were, of course, a peace church and objected to all war. Jud said, "I would never be able to live in a country and refuse to defend it!"

We talked for hours, comparing our beliefs with Jud's Catholic background. Jud's small group tried to explain our church's position but also asked Jud to tell us about the Catholics. Finally one evening Jud said, "I wish you would stop asking me about my Catholic roots. I know much more about the Anabaptists than I ever knew about Catholics!"

Conversion came to Jud in many ways. His relationship to Pam was also transformed and made new. Soon Jud was taking the membership class and in a few months, on a glorious Sunday morning, he was baptized into our church family.

As important as the longtime members are, I am often reminded that it is the new person joining the church that brings new life, joy, and renewal. At Jud's baptism he read a wonderful letter of his feelings on this special day:

> I would like to thank the whole congregation for your support and acceptance of me into the church. These past days I keep thinking about my past experiences on my uncle's farm in Pennsylvania. My brother and I used to spend our summers there fishing and working on the farm.
> We'd work from sunup to sundown and at the end of the long day we'd be tired and weary. To clean ourselves off we would go swimming in a mountain stream that ran the length of the farm. It was simply a beautiful swimming hole, with moss-covered rocks, mountain laurel, and water so clear it was crystal blue.
> After swimming we were so refreshed and alive that we felt we could go do the chores all over again.
> I've been looking for a feeling similar to this to refresh my soul. I tried several things, all of which were short-lived, false renewers of life. Not until I started attending Warwick River Church did I find the beautiful renewing feeling Christ can bring into my life. I love every one of you beautiful people. —May 3, 1987.

Create in me a clean heart, O God,
    and put a new and right spirit within me.
    Do not cast me away from your presence,
    and do not take your holy spirit from me.
    —Psalm 51:10-11

9

North Meets South

*"We start to trust a person
when he starts sounding like us."*

When I accepted my first assignment as pastor at a Pennsylvania church, it dawned on me how "funny" everyone talked. Apparently, funny worked both ways. I learned that our English language as spoken south of the Mason Dixon line was not always understood by northern listeners. And vice-versa—the words and phrases spoken in my new community sometimes sounded like they were a foreign language.

I heard stories of other ministers and how they too faced the hazards of public speaking as they moved around the country.

For instance, my Uncle George R. Brunk was a well-known and well-traveled evangelist. He delivered his message with the power of conviction and a strong southern accent. While holding meetings in Canada, he told his audience how he felt about those who try to live the Christian life without looking to the Holy Spirit for guidance. He proclaimed emphatically, "I wouldn't give a dime for that kind of religion!"

Immediately after the service, a local brother came to him and said, "We don't usually use that kind of strong language here." Puzzled, George asked what he had said that was offensive. The man replied, "You said you don't give a damn for that kind of religion." At the very next service, Uncle George explained to his listeners that he was trying to say he wouldn't give ten cents for that kind of Christianity.

I learned that the language we speak can be a great distraction. At lunch one Sunday, my host told me she liked it when I said, "Please open your Bobbles." I would rather have heard that she caught some new revelation or came to some new appreciation for the Scriptures!

An elderly Pennsylvania couple spoke with such a strong Pennsylvania Dutch accent that I had a hard time understanding them. It was not just the accent but also the phrasing. One day Lewie asked me, "Brother Truman, did you ever have the homesick?"

Then he went on to explain how homesick his wife had been in the early years of their marriage, how hard it was for her to leave her parents and move away to live with Lewie. She "had the homesick something awful."

One morning after church, Lewie waited until we were alone and he said, "Brother Truman, I'm sorry for giving you the horn this morning." I was puzzled and asked him to explain. Apparently he was following a slow driver on the way to church and in frustration blew the horn. When both cars turned into the church parking lot, Lewie caught on who the slow driver was.

After five years in Pennsylvania, a man who had become my friend told me, "We start to trust a person when he starts to sound like us." So I worked hard to change my "dialect." I made even more effort to pronounce all my R's and to polish up my best "northern" accent.

If the goal is better communication and bridge-building, then the change is worth the extra effort.

10

Not an Answer but a Presence

Doris was perhaps the most mature Christian I have ever known.

In my first month at Akron Mennonite Church in Pennsylvania, Doris called from her home in Kansas. Doris Janzen Longacre was a member of the Akron congregation who was working on a Masters in Nutrition at Kansas State University.

She explained that her cancer had reappeared, and the prognosis was not good. Doris and her family were making plans to return to Pennsylvania and would soon be back in their home church.

She let me know that she needed a pastor who could pray, believing that she would be healed. Doris asked, "Truman, do you believe in prayer?" I assured her that yes, I did believe in prayer. I knew that I would have to grow stronger in my faith.

Doris lived for two more years after moving back to Pennsylvania. She made a huge contribution in so many ways. She lived her life with a heart tuned to the needs of developing countries. From her years in Vietnam and Indonesia with Mennonite Central Committee (MCC), she and husband Paul had learned about poverty and hunger.

As the person who initiated the *More-with-Less Cookbook*, Doris wrote in the preface, "We are looking for ways to live more simply and joyfully, ways that grow out of our tradition but take their shape from living faith and the demands of our hungry world."

The book received broad acceptance, churchwide and far beyond. (Tens of thousands of dollars of *More-with-Less Cookbook* royalties have gone directly to MCC for world hunger.)

Doris was a leader in the congregation. One Sunday morning she preached a sermon that lived on long after her death. In her presentation entitled "Not an Answer but a Presence," she gave a brief glimpse into her recent past.

She explained, "Two years ago we took a study leave from MCC. We intended to go to graduate school. Actually, we ended up going to two schools. One of these was Kansas State University. The other was a school with a much more difficult curriculum—the school for finding God's presence in the experience of having cancer."

At an anointing service for Doris we reminded her, "It is not our big faith that heals. It is our Big God who brings healing and hope." Doris learned to embrace her pain. She practiced the stewardship of pain. Because of her, I have learned to pay attention to pain in personal stories and in Bible stories.

Doris was a pioneer in spiritual formation, journaling, prayer and fasting, meditation and reflection. All through her illness she kept a journal and she shared her writings with me. She wanted contact with God.

She wrote, "I found that I have an *innermost*. I needed the light of God's presence; otherwise my aloneness would lead to loneliness. Psalm 42:1-2 expresses my cry, 'As the hart longs for flowing streams, so longs my soul for thee, O God. My soul thirsts for God, for the living God. When shall I come and behold the face of God?'"

There were many places where Doris struggled with God. She said, "Wrestle with God! Struggle with God! It is better to offend him than to ignore him!" Her journal reflects this life-and-death struggle.

From Doris I received so much more than I gave. I think of her when I read these words by Sue Monk Kidd: "If you can't be still and wait, you can't become what God created you to be." Doris did a lot of waiting and her soul grew up. She was perhaps the most mature Christian I have ever known.

11

The Gift of Affirmation

The beaming child was thriving on my approval.

The service was over and benediction prayed. I was at the back of the church shaking hands. This was a relaxing time for me—the sermon delivered, the many details of the morning completed. I enjoyed greeting the members individually.

The next person holding out her hand was tiny little Becky. She looked particularly charming this morning, and I exclaimed, "Becky, you have such a lovely dress, and you are so beautiful!" She beamed back at me.

I went on shaking hands. Some folks said the message had been meaningful. Some said they would call for an appointment later in the week. I enjoyed the interaction and feedback.

But here came Becky again, beaming all the more beautifully! I told her again how lovely she was, how beautiful her dress, and what a neat little girl she was.

When Becky came through the line the third time, I started to catch on. The child was thriving on my approval!

I was reminded again how much all of us need to hear kind words of affirmation. People come to church for a whole variety of reasons. First of all, it is hoped, we come to receive heavenly food, to be nourished in our faith, and to renew our covenants with God and God's people. We also come to be affirmed and loved by our spiritual brothers and sisters, fathers and mothers.

Every congregation has people who are lonely, unloved, unaffirmed, never touched. God's people need each other! We might even need to hear, "You are looking especially lovely today." Wouldn't God want us to speak well of God's creation? Can't we do this for each other in the family of God?

I am reminded of a song by Ken Medema, "If This Is Not a Place," in which he captures the kind of refuge a church needs to be. A place where questions can be asked. Where tears are understood. Where blessing is given and received. This is the kind of church that I need.

> *Mark 10:14-16.* [Jesus said], "Let the little children come to me, and do not hinder them, for the kingdom of God belongs to such as these. I tell you the truth, anyone who will not receive the kingdom of God like a little child will never enter it." And he took the children in his arms, put his hands on them and blessed them.

12

A Letter from Liz

*Her wounds were as fresh
as if they had happened yesterday.*

Liz and her children had been attending our church for a number of months. She seemed unusually intelligent, bright, and pleasant to be with. She was attractive, too. My wife and I thought she looked like Elizabeth Taylor. We wondered what her story was, and if she had a husband.

One day we received word in the church office that Liz was in the hospital. Apparently some medical tests had raised questions about the possibility of cancer and further testing was needed. As usual, if any member or church attender was in the hospital, in my role as pastor I would go to visit.

I tapped on her hospital door. Liz said, "Hello, Truman. I have just been writing you a letter." She read aloud the message she was wording. "Please do not come and see me in the hospital. I have never had a good relationship with a pastor or a bishop, so why should I expect one now?"

I stammered, embarrassed at the intrusion, backed out of the room as gracefully as possible, and found my way out of the hospital. On the way home, I felt like bawling. Humiliation! What had ever made me think I could be a pastor? How could I get out of the ministry?

By the time I had driven the ten miles back to my office, I had pulled myself together. This was the first time I had been so blatantly brushed off. As bad as it hurt, there was a valuable lesson to be learned. My church might be full of people like Liz who had been hurt by earlier experiences.

I learned later that Liz had grown up in a strict church where rules were more important than relationships. She had been bitterly disappointed. Her wounds were as fresh as if they had happened yesterday. It would take years for her to get past these hurts.

Some people seem to survive the strictness of their religious backgrounds and are able to forgive and forget. Others need a long time to heal. Liz perceived me as a link to every pastor, every bishop, she had ever known.

Eventually Liz returned to church and we began to build a positive relationship. This was an early lesson for me. I have worked hard throughout my ministry to restore those who have been broken by rules that were too severe.

"There's a wideness in God's mercy. . . ."

13

My Bargain with Winfield

*I agreed to call him when
we invited a woman to preach.*

At every church I served, a few good men became good friends. Often a little older than I, they could be trusted to be honest with me as I entered a new church and community.

Winfield was one of these friends. He ran a successful lumberyard a few miles from the church. I enjoyed visiting him in his rough shed/office where he wrote orders and managed the business. On a cold day, his woodstove, stocked with pieces of slab wood from the yard, provided a great place to warm myself and catch up with everyday happenings.

In this cozy setting one cold morning, Winfield, ever the gentleman, eased into a conversation to let me know his true feelings about women in ministry. He explained, "Truman, when you have a woman in the pulpit it makes me very uncomfortable. In fact, I feel like I am sinning even to sit there in the congregation and listen to a woman preacher." He quoted Scripture to back up his beliefs.

I did not want to lose ground on this important issue of inviting women into the pulpit. Most of the church members were accepting this new development, and I had expected some to object.

Not wanting an argument, I thought for a minute and then replied,

"How about making a deal? When we have scheduled a woman to speak, I will call you early in the week and you can visit the Presbyterian church that Sunday."

Winfield agreed to this arrangement. For the next few years I would call and "warn" him when we had invited a woman preacher. Then one day I said to him, "We always publicize our preaching schedule some weeks in advance. I would like you to watch for yourself and decide when to stay away from our services." He seemed satisfied with this.

When I retired from this church and moved back to Virginia, the search committee invited a couple, Paul and Grace, to come as interim pastors. A husband-and-wife team where the woman would do half the preaching! Several months later I learned to my great relief and joy that Winfield loved Grace's preaching. He never missed a Sunday when it was Grace's turn to preach.

14

Singing All the Way Home

His son called to say that the end was near.

Vernon loved his home church. He had attended it for more than fifty years. Here his children had been baptized and their weddings hosted. Brothers and sisters and nieces and nephews and grandchildren were members here. He had expected to worship here the rest of his life.

But things were changing, and Vernon was not happy with the changes. He loved the old hymns of the church. It ruined his Sunday when he heard only guitars and off-the-wall music. Vernon did not feel at home anymore.

It took a lot of courage for Vernon and Anne finally to give up on their home church. It meant they had to leave behind many old friends and even family members.

They started coming to the neighboring Blooming Glen church where I was pastor. As they made the switch, other family members followed. This was a gifted family, and their attendance was a huge benefit to Blooming Glen. We were blessed, honored, and strengthened by their many contributions.

Soon Vernon was asked to become the Sunday school teacher for the oldest class in our church. He was a born teacher, and the class responded warmly. He was more than a teacher to them; he was a friend and informal pastor as well. He and Anne called on class members with health problems. They ministered to the large class in so many ways.

When Vernon was diagnosed with a terminal illness, it was a blow to the many people he cared for. He remained active and optimistic as he battled his disease. We all prayed for a miracle but the disease did not go away. We finally had to accept the fact that Vernon would be leaving us.

The evening came when his son called to say that the end was near. He asked me to come and join the family. Vernon lay on a hospital bed in the dining room. His sons and their families were with him. His beloved Anne was by his side. Vernon comforted those around him saying, "God has promised eternal life—not just for a time but forever!"

The family spent the evening singing, crying, and sometimes laughing. They spoke words of love to Vernon. Son Michael led one of his dad's favorite hymns, "I have a song that Jesus gave me. . . . In my heart there rings a melody." Even Vernon sang along.

At one point I leaned over Vernon and prayed for him and for the family. Vernon opened his eyes and said, "Truman, you could have picked a prettier tie for this occasion!" Of course we all chuckled. Vernon was too much!

The very next day, Vernon left for his eternal home. I will never forget my friend, Vernon Bishop.

15

On Keeping the Main Thing the Main Thing

"What will happen if we choose the boat?"

Tom came home from work all excited and asked Dorine, "Did you see the boat for sale down the street? It's just what I've been looking for! It's just the right size! The right price! Half the price of a new boat! It's a steal!"

Dorine had indeed seen the boat and the sign. She stood in the doorway to the kitchen and responded, "When would you play with the new boat? In the two hours you're home Saturday afternoon? Or your three hours of free time on Sunday?"

Tom watched her turn her back and head for the kitchen as she hurled her parting shot: "You'll have to choose—it's me or the boat!" Frankie, age six, watched the interaction. He looked up at his dad, man to man, and said, "What will happen if we choose the boat?"

Tom and Dorine and Sallie and Frankie were a family I loved and admired. The parents were hardworking, gifted, talented, and fun-loving. The children were bright and lively.

Like so many other young families, their days were packed full. Amid all their other obligations, they managed to make significant contributions to the church family.

We know that young couples (and older folks too) are under tremendous pressure. Credit cards invite us to overspend. We slip into the belief that one more possession, one more vacation, one more THING will bring happiness. We must discover for ourselves that all the possessions in the world will not satisfy this hunger. Only God can satisfy.

About this time, a number of couples were asking for a class on this very subject—how to prioritize time and energies so that they could live their lives with kingdom values.

We decided to offer a Wednesday evening class, using Stephen Covey's *The Seven Habits of Highly Effective Families*. We met for four Wednesday evenings. Tom and Dorene turned their problem into a "challenge" that helped other couples who were making similar decisions. And the boat issue was solved to the satisfaction of both.

By the end of the series, each of the families had written their own mission statement and placed it on the refrigerator door as a visible reminder. I still have copies of those mission statements. And I hope that some of the families still look back and remember their family's true values from that stage in life.

16

My Friend Elmer

*He was a pillar in his
home and a pillar in our church.*

Before I arrived at Blooming Glen church in Pennsylvania, I had been told by Overseer Paul M. Lederach, "Truman, you will not run the church. The elders will do that. You will be free to preach, visit the sick, marry the couples, and dedicate the babies. You will not need to run the church."

I wasn't sure what I thought of this. It was certainly not the way we did things in Virginia. But I came to appreciate the arrangement and learned to love churches with well-trained elders. Blooming Glen took eldership seriously. I remember the dedication of these outstanding men and women.

Elmer Yoder was one of these committed people. An early retiree from Procter and Gamble, he was a capable leader. Elmer had been a member at Blooming Glen for thirty years, ever since he came east to marry Ruth, a daughter of the church. He seemed to know the soul of the congregation and was highly respected by fellow members. When discipline was called for, Elmer was wise and diplomatic.

Over months and years Elmer and Ruth became our close friends. On Sunday evenings we would relax over wedding soup at Zotos or pizza at The Spotted Hog. We felt blessed.

Once on a trip to Kansas, out of respect for Elmer, we decided to visit his place of birth. We located pinpoints on the map for Elmer, Kansas, and for Yoder, Kansas. At Yoder, we found a bustling Amish community. We ate lunch at an Amish restaurant.

Then we drove on to Elmer, Kansas, which was still on the map, but the town was dead. What had been a little railroad town was all boarded-up. Back in Pennsylvania we had fun reporting to Elmer our Kansas sightseeing tour.

One day, out of the blue, Elmer wrecked his car. Something was wrong; he was not himself. In the days that followed, Elmer sometimes reverted to Pennsylvania Dutch, the language of his childhood. He went to see specialists in Philadelphia, and it was determined that he would need brain surgery.

We went often to see Elmer at the University of Pennsylvania Hospital. We prayed; the whole church prayed for his healing. But Elmer had a massive stroke and died. His beloved Ruth, along with daughter Michelle and son Chad, stood at his bedside and shed tears of grief and disappointment.

How do you go on living when your rock has been removed from your side? Elmer was a pillar in his home and a pillar in our church. Elmer, I still think of you often and miss you. You were a wonderful friend.

17

Angels in the Pulpit

*On that Sunday morning,
there had been two sightings.*

"If we really knew what can happen in worship, we would wear seat belts and crash helmets." I can't remember where this line came from. It might have been written by Madeleine L'Engle.

Have you ever been in a worship service when you felt you needed some protection?

At Blooming Glen church, the worship committee planned "Lay Sunday" every fall. The pastors could sit with their families and enjoy the morning service without having any special responsibility. It was always a rewarding and unusual happening. The call to worship, congregational singing, offertory, sermon, prayers, and benediction all were done by lay members.

What a blessed experience to be among the "normal parishioners" and just take it all in. On one particular Lay Sunday, the assignments had been spread out among a whole host of men and women and young people. Many shared their gifts in the various parts of the service.

Three people preached the morning message. We felt the Holy Spirit's presence.

When the service was over and the Sunday school classes formed, teachers began to hear from their students: A little girl said to her teacher, "I saw an angel up in the front!" Upstairs in the oldest class, one of the members told the group, "You know, I saw an angel behind each speaker this morning!"

Sightings of angels were rare in our congregation. But on that Sunday morning, there had been two sightings! That morning at Blooming Glen remains a vivid memory.

I believe that two groups of people are likely to experience miracles: the very young and the very old. More than any other time, at these periods in life our hearts seem tuned in and listening.

I want to be aware of angels. Make me like young Samuel or like old Simeon. Praise God! I want to see and hear God.

> *Acts 5:19-20.* During the night an angel of the Lord opened the doors of the jail and brought them out. "Go, stand in the temple courts," he said, "and tell the people the full message of this new life."

18

Who's Afraid of Marriage Enrichment?

*We will never forget what
the elderly husband shared with the group.*

"I feel loved and valued when . . . you laugh at my jokes." "I feel understood when . . . you get up in the middle of the night to check out the strange noise that woke me up."

Responding to questions, questions, questions. This is hard work! A whole page of questions! Is this supposed to be a test? She knows I love her. I told her that when we got married.

When our children were young, we attended our first marriage enrichment weekend, led by Abe and Dorothy Schmitt, at our church in Harrisonburg, Virginia. It was hard work trying to focus on the specific questions being asked. And we felt the need to be careful, not wanting to hurt each others' feelings.

We had to learn how to complete the line that said, "Do you understand that I love you and that I would appreciate. . . ?" We were asked to think of something that we wanted from our partner that would make our good marriage even better.

That first weekend was rewarding. We learned things about each other that we could never have learned without the help of the leaders and the "test papers."

We learned from other members in the group. After couples had a chance to answer their questions and process them with each other, the group would be called together to share openly as much as they cared to. Some in the group were more comfortable with this step than others. They liked the storytelling better than the writing.

Later Betty and I traveled to Wilmore, Kentucky, to train as marriage enrichment leaders. The trainer was preacher and author David Seamands. We had learned to know and appreciate him when he came to Eastern Mennonite College as guest speaker for Spiritual Life Week.

In a comfortable lodge setting, each evening David and his wife Helen sat together on the sofa telling some of the playful, earthy stories of their own relationship. We still remember some of their provocative or romantic or funny reports. They were great role models.

For more than twenty years, we accepted invitations to lead marriage enrichment weekends. Usually these experiences were good for renewing our own appreciation for each other as well. We learned fun things from the participants.

How could we ever forget the elderly couple who had been married for fifty years? He wrote (and later shared with the group), "I am saying I love and appreciate you when . . . I lay out your nightie each night." How romantic can you get? This man of seventy goes to his wife's dresser and chooses her nightgown! He was such a good sport for letting us younger men hear this sentimental secret.

If you are a married couple and have never taken a marriage enrichment weekend, please do so at the first opportunity! You will have fun, you will learn so much you need to know about your spouse, and about yourself. It's nothing to be afraid of!

19

Family Sculpting with Virginia Satir

The "mother" and "father" and "son" greeted and hugged each other!

It was a great privilege to attend Virginia Satir's Seminar sponsored by Family Service Delaware in Wilmington, Delaware.

In the 1980s my wife Betty worked at Family Service Lancaster, Pennsylvania, and I was pastor at Akron Mennonite Church. Every once in awhile we found continuing education opportunities that would benefit both of us, and it was fun to attend together.

When the brochure arrived, both of us knew this would be a chance of a lifetime. We had well-marked books in our library by Virginia Satir: *Peoplemaking* and *Conjoint Family Therapy*. The workshop setting would be the beautiful Du Pont Country Club. So we arranged our work schedules and looked forward to a day of renewal.

According to the flyer, the topics to be addressed were: "Family Mapping" (or sculpting) and "Honoring Individual Needs in the Family."

We arrived in time for registration and coffee (in china cups). Then, along with about three hundred other social-worker types, we made our way to the ballroom where the morning session was to be held.

Virginia Satir was a most energetic speaker. She immediately got all of us involved in a joining exercise. We knew right away that we would be participants, not spectators. That was alright with me. I was eager to learn more from her demonstrations.

First she described how she goes about family sculpting with a troubled family. She explained the importance of being clear and straight with the family, the importance of each one connecting with the other, and how to help the family reconstruct when barriers have been set up.

And then Virginia Satir pointed to me and said, "I would like you to come to the platform. You will be the father. Then she pointed to three others: "You will be the mother, you will be the son in the family, and you the daughter."

So now I was on the platform with the famous Virginia Satir about to meet my "wife" and "children." The woman stepping into the ring had big bright eyes and a vivacious smile. She looked familiar to me. As the son stepped forward, he too, looked like someone I had known in the past.

With Satir guiding the action, we role-played the troubled family situations: Who is on the outside looking in? Who is standing in the middle as a peacemaker? Who is the focus of all the attention? Who is standing on the edge of the circle with one foot barely touching the circle?

When the exercise was over, Satir dismissed us to go back to our seats. Betty recalls what happened next. The "mother" and "father" and "son" greeted and hugged each other! Betty thought this was carrying things a little too far. It took awhile for all of us to realize that three of the "family members" were old Eastern Mennonite University (EMU) acquaintances!

It was a memorable day. When you attend a church college, you make hundreds of new friends and in some way you become members of a large family. And if you are fortunate, years later you will run into these friends at the least expected times. The networking goes on and on. We got more than we expected that day when Virginia Satir sculpted an EMU "family."

20

Finding Myself in Hot Water

I have tried to help those who have been wounded by the church.

Recently a quote from G. K. Chesterton grabbed my attention. I wrote it down for future reference: "I believe in getting into hot water; it keeps you clean."

Getting into hot water is not a comfortable place to be. Only a few times in my ministry have I really been aware of standing at "a different place" from the majority of fellow ministers in my conference. But isn't being in hot water preferable to going against one's own convictions?

When I was younger, I was more convinced about what was "right" and "wrong." For instance, I was not open to the possibility of performing a second marriage when the first marriage partner was still living.

If a Mennonite couple found themselves in a divorce situation, they simply had to quit attending church. At the time when they most needed the support of a caring community, they found themselves without a church family. Pastors who began to counsel and support and care for divorcing couples, found themselves in hot water with their conference or district.

The Mennonite church is important to me. And it is in my nature to be in agreement whenever possible with my group of fellow-believers. But there are times when I would like to say to those in my church, "Wake up! Let's get on with important questions! Let's not major in minor issues!"

How many conferences and committees have been devoted to casting out persons who cannot conform to our mold? The Bible seems to say, "Open your arms to those who are different and don't easily conform to your ways of being."

For most of my ministry I have tried to help those who have been wounded by the church. Some are hurt so severely that they never recover. Some are forever outside the church and its influence.

This leads me to the desire to be compassionate and cautious about passing judgment. I do not want to be part of the wounding process.

The older I get, the more I realize the need for a "nonjudgmental presence." Those who are different need pastoral care and love. They deserve to be listened to.

Aren't we to be compassionate as our Father in heaven is compassionate? Relationships matter to me. I would choose gentleness, kindness, longsuffering, forgiveness, and understanding. I would not want to cause further suffering to those who find themselves "different" from the mainstream. I would rather err on the side of grace.

Is it too much to hope for a church that opens her arms to those who are "different"? These are the people who need pastoral care and support, maybe even more than the general membership. They need a welcoming church. I long to be part of such a church family.

21

Continuing Education

Sometimes these staid Presbyterian pastors rose to their feet in a standing ovation.

When one is preaching and teaching and visiting the sick month after month, year after year, how does a pastor keep his own spirit fresh and excited about the ministry?

During my years at Blooming Glen Mennonite Church, in Bucks County, Pennsylvania, it was my privilege to be within an hour's drive of Princeton Seminary in New Jersey.

I kept the Princeton catalog at my fingertips. Every couple of months I would set out early Monday morning to attend some special conference or workshop. Sometimes I would take in a weeklong conference with a favorite author: Herbert O'Driscoll, Diogenes Allen, Frederick Buechner, Barbara Brown Taylor, or Frederick Dale Bruner.

All of these author/speakers were inspiring; I would return home refreshed. Dale Bruner is one teacher I remember appreciatively. A small man with an intense passion for Bible study, he grew up attending Hollywood Presbyterian Church and often mentioned a special Bible teacher, Henrietta C. Mears, who loved the Bible and inspired her students to do the same.

During Bruner's student years at Princeton, he became interested in the work of the Holy Spirit. Trying to understand the Pentecostal movement, he attended Pentecostal churches, conferences, and prayer meetings. He read the literature and talked with church leaders.

Bruner explained that he did not look only for head knowledge about the Spirit. He wanted his teaching to embrace both the head and the heart. He spoke of

Spiritual depth,
   Social width,
      Eucharistic height,
         And prayerful length.

I learned from Dale Bruner the concept of spiritual saturation. This involved immersing my mind in the Word and allowing the Scripture to "marinate" my brain and heart. Bruner taught that to believe in Christ *is* the filling of the Spirit, and every new draft of faith in the Savior is a fresh filling of the Spirit.

Bruner liked to teach the old-fashioned way—a verse at a time. His presentation would climb to a crescendo and remain up in the air with excitement. By the time he ended, sometimes these staid Presbyterian pastors would rise to their feet in a standing ovation.

I loved my trips to Princeton. The hour-long drive across the Delaware River, through small towns and countryside, then entering the wide boulevard lined with ancient, peeling sycamore trees—this was renewal itself. And I would return home blessed, feeling a new infilling of the Holy Spirit.

22

When the Heart Waits (*Sermon*)

Out of the shadows, the old man walked toward the little family.

The gospel story today is about two devout people
    who waited for Jesus to come.
        Come with me and enter this Christmas story:

The old man Simeon came to the temple
    hundreds of times
        without seeing Jesus.

There must have been days when his faith wavered,
    when the voice of promise
seemed little more than
    whistling in the dark,
        a pious dream without foundation.

Simeon must have said to himself a thousand times,
    "I'll never give up!"
He kept clinging to the promise,
    taking leaps of faith into the darkness.
He kept coming to the end of his rope.
    He would feel despair and hopelessness.

But then he would
    tie a knot at the end of the rope
        And keep hanging on.

He would not give up!
    He kept his vision—and nurtured it.
He never lost his dream.
    And one day the miracle took place.
        It was a day like all the others,
            a day of watching and longing.

The doors of the temple opened!
    Mary and Joseph and baby Jesus entered!
        Simeon knew immediately!
Here was the Christ child!
    The Messiah!
Out of the shadows the old man
    walked toward the little family.

Simeon took the baby in his arms.
    Filled with the Holy Spirit,
        in deep devotion Simeon whispered,
"Salvation! Salvation!"
Simeon gathered strength,
    and spoke louder,
lifting the baby high for all to see.

Then he cried out,
"Salvation!
Salvation for all people!
    A light, a light
        to lighten all people!
            The glory of the Lord is revealed!"

The artist Giotto captured the moment:
    Simeon, holding the baby high in the air
        and over the altar.
    The baby reaching for mother Mary.

For Giotto it is the beginning of the road to the cross.
　Over the whole painting is the shadow of the cross.

The Holy Spirit was with Simeon,
　upon him like a dove,
　　revealing Jesus to him.

Simeon was a righteous man.
　He was in right relationship with God,
　　at peace, striving to do good.

Simeon was devout.
　He took his faith seriously and
　　lived a holy life.

Simeon praised God,
　a holy man who could lift his arms in praise.

Simeon had eyes that saw the salvation of the Lord.
　Some believe that,
　　until Jesus came,
　　　Simeon had limited eyesight.
　　　　But now he saw Jesus clearly.

Simeon blessed the little Holy Family,
　extended his hands to them and blessed them.

Not only was Simeon waiting.
　Also standing there in the temple was Anna.
She too waited and waited and waited,
　never giving up.
　　Was Anna eighty years old?
　　Or was she 103?

Nobody knows.
　But at this very moment she entered the picture,
　　well up in years,
　　　never leaving the temple courts.
Worshiping day and night,
　fasting and praying without ceasing,
　　waiting for the redemption of Jerusalem.

In constant touch with God,
she spent a lot of time listening to God.
Anna shared her faith.
She talked about Jesus with every person she met.
Her faith was contagious.

This is a story about keeping the faith.
The Holy Spirit is very active at the birth of Jesus.
Over and over in the narrative
Luke points to the Holy Spirit.

Simeon and Anna knew how to wait.
Not in a passive way.
Waiting for them was a spiritual discipline.

In Sue Monk Kidd's book, *When the Heart Waits* (HarperSan Francisco, 1992) she writes, "When you're waiting, you're not doing nothing. You're doing the most important something there is. You're allowing your soul to grow up. If you can't be still and wait, you can't become what God created you to be" (p. 22).

Both Simeon and Anna are "God-receivers."
They wait with open arms,
ready to receive the Christ-child.
They take his little soft hands
into their old, gnarled hands.
They touch the child's softness.
They pat the baby lovingly.
The baby is comfortable in their arms.
Jesus knows he is loved!

The baby is blessed by Simeon and Anna.
When Jesus is blessed
and when the parents are blessed,
They leave the temple singing.
They have the mantle of blessing on them!

Note the spiritual disciplines in this passage:
Filled with the Spirit,

waiting and watching,
*   listening, slowing down,*
*   serving, praying, fasting,*
*   paying attention.*

Hungering and thirsting,
*   being still,*
*   persisting,*
*   giving thanks,*
*   touching, blessing.*

We remember that we are created
*   like Simeon and Anna,*
*   to receive God.*

Could we "turn the heat up a notch"
*   from warm to hot?*
Could we step up our passion for God?
*   Living a life centered on God and God's Word,*
*   being a "receiver of Christ,"*
continuing to be transformed into the likeness of Christ?

Like Simeon and Anna, let us be in a spirit of
*   waiting and watching.*
*   The baby has come.*
*   The Messiah has come!*

Amen.

Part 3
LOVE MY SHEEP

Introduction

Once more, there are sheep in the meadow behind our home. They would be lost if somebody didn't remember to take care of them. I need to fill the water trough, pour out the grain, provide a green field and dry shelter. It is fun to think of the many ways that a shepherd is like a pastor.

Retirement is a challenge. Some have spoken about climbing down the ladder. For me, that picture does not work. I like the idea of jumping off the ladder from the top. What exhilaration!

I have been inspired by the work of Frederick Buechner. I first heard him speak at Princeton Theological Seminary, and I liked the way he explored such topics as faith, hope, and love. In *A Room Called Remember* (Harper & Row, 1984), Buechner describes well the place where I now find myself:

> In the room called Remember it is possible to find peace—the peace that comes from looking back and remembering to remember that . . . we were never really alone. We could never have made it this far. (p. 8)

Countless stories and testimonies come to mind and feed my soul. Only a few are recorded here. They are the stories of saints and sinners, all prodigals come home to God's embrace.

In remembering, the word that stands out is *Welcome.* God is a Big God who accepts, forgives, and redeems his children. I see ever more clearly what God has been about since creation.

Let these words soak into me: Welcome, Open Arms, Forgiveness, Redemption, Peace. I want to live like Jesus. Yes, there is still work to do. And like Jesus I want to say to younger ministers: "Greater work will you do. Your stories will build the kingdom and help us celebrate God's work in the world today."

1

Love My Sheep

*While snow was still
on the ground, the baby lambs were born.*

Spring stood out in the crowded pasture. She was a Scottish black-face sheep. She had been raised as a pet with the farmer's family and would much rather trail after the sheepdog than identify with the other ninety and nine.

We had recently moved to a property with a barn, an acre of land, and a fenced-in hillside that would provide the ideal setting for a few sheep. We spoke to Farmer Charlie, and he agreed to let us have Spring and her two lambs. It was our plan to produce our own lambs by the following year.

We knew when we bought the place that we did not want to mow the steep hillside. It would be so much simpler and cheaper and more eco-friendly to stock it with sheep. (Wrong! Sheep are not simpler or cheaper. They are a lot of trouble and they are expensive.)

Cousin Rowland helped get the fence mended and the water access ready. When the place was ready, Charles delivered Spring and her two "teenagers" as we called them. They quickly adjusted to their new surroundings. We enjoyed watching them from our kitchen window. They provided the pastoral scene we had dreamed of.

To keep on plan, we had Charlie bring a gentleman caller. The three females would "baa" as he stalked them. It was a pretty amazing sight and caused some excitement in our quiet neighborhood of retired folk.

Soon we had three pregnant sheep. We took extra good care of them. We eagerly awaited the delivery dates. In March, while snow was still on the ground, the baby lambs were born. On three successive Sundays, about 8 o'clock in the morning, a neighbor called to report that a sheep was in labor. I would call Charles (as previously arranged) and he would come. He knew exactly what to do.

Spring herself gave birth to twins, and each of the "teenagers" had single births. This meant that seven sheep were now in our fields. We thought up names for the lambs but then decided that really the mothers should name their babies.

So we listened carefully over the next weeks until we learned the names of our four baby lambs. They were Ma-aa-ggy and P-ee-achy and Ba-am-bi and Ma-aa-ndy. We think the first two were nicknames for Magnolia and Peach Blossom, since it was that time of year.

The lambs were absolutely adorable. We were thrilled with our farm animals. They became the center of attraction for neighbors and visiting grandchildren. A friend took a picture of me in the pasture feeding the flock. I was so proud of the photo showing me taking care of the sheep. I took the photo and made Christmas cards and printed the words, "Rejoice! I have found my sheep!"

That Christmas card is our favorite of all we have ever sent. And it became the door to another whole experience, but that is another story.

2

Feed My Sheep

*They are grabby and pushy
and can cause a lot of trouble.*

We had so much fun watching our three adult sheep and their four lambkins. Others seemed to enjoy them, too. Sometimes we would look out the window and see the neighborhood children lined up along the fence, just watching the antics and playfulness of the babies. If it was close to feeding time, I would take the small bucket of corn and feed the sheep. It was amusing to watch the sheep nudge and push each other aside to see who could get the biggest share.

One afternoon when I went out to give the sheep their evening meal, their plastic troughs had blown down the hill. I walked through the gate with the bucket of corn, heading for the troughs.

When the sheep realized I had all that good stuff in the little bucket, they rushed me. I tried to step away quickly and started to run. Running downhill is quite an experience for a man my age. The sheep and I seemed to be going a hundred miles an hour. We didn't stop until we got to the barn, where I fell flat, spreadeagled on the rocky ground.

If only I had stopped in my tracks and just set down the bucket of corn, this story wouldn't even be a story. The sheep would have devoured their supper and I would have walked like a gentleman farmer back to the house. Instead, I worked my way back up the hill and into the house, bleeding and bruised. The fingers on my right hand pointed in four different directions. What a bloody mess!

I called for Betty and told her she needed to get me to the hospital. She took a second to assess the situation and said that she couldn't possibly drive me to the hospital. I would need to call 911. This did not appeal to me, so I asked her if she would call my sister Sandy and have her come. Sandy agreed that we needed to call the ambulance.

We received quick attention at the hospital. One pregnant nurse turned her head away and told me she could not look at me or she would be sick. The ER doctor predicted that I had at least three broken bones. X-rays however showed no broken bones, just four badly displaced fingers.

The doctor explained that if only one or two fingers were dislocated he could put them back in place, but with four out of place, he would need to put me to sleep. That was fine with me.

For the next weeks and months I visited a physical therapist. I gained new appreciation for physical therapists, or occupational therapists as they are called when they focus on the hand and wrist. My therapist was named Terri. She was so caring and knowledgeable and knew what to do to get the hand and fingers to start working again.

I have to admit that this episode caused me to change my opinion of sheep. I know they have a reputation for being sweet and gentle, and they look wonderful on Christmas cards. But they do have another side. They are grabby and pushy and can cause a lot of trouble.

3

Sheep Pictures

*On the front wall
was the one Betty wanted.*

When we accepted an interim pastorate in Neffsville, Pennsylvania, we had to let our sheep go back to the farmer. We fully intended to rebuild our flock the following spring, but before we had a chance to get the sheep back, we had accepted a call from a second church.

Meanwhile, we were lonesome for our sheep and were drawn to fields of sheep. We traveled in Switzerland and Germany and learned how to go into gift shops asking for *schaf*. Mostly the shopkeepers did not understand what we were asking for.

While we were interim pastors at Neffsville Mennonite Church, Betty went calling on a member facing health issues. She had barely stepped into the living room when her eyes fell on a painting of sheep. She said to the lady of the house, "I have to get a painting like that for Truman." And Dorothy replied, "You can get one just like this one here in Lancaster, at the Suk Shuglie Gallery on Manheim Pike."

That Friday afternoon, just as soon as we could leave the church office, we drove to find the gallery. Now that we have learned to know Suk, she recalls how that visit went. According to Suk, Betty came into the gallery asking, "Do you have a painting of sheep?"

Suk had lots of paintings of sheep, and on the front wall was the one Betty wanted, exactly like the one on Dorothy's wall. We left the studio that day with a large framed print, and hung it on the wall of the pastor's study at the church.

That was the first of many, many visits to Suk's gallery. We went there often on a Friday afternoon, calling it our "attitude adjustment hour." We relaxed and learned to know Suk as a gentle, loving, very talented artist. One Friday we took her a copy of the Christmas card we had sent out several years earlier, a photo of us feeding our sheep. We explained that we too have a love for sheep and that we had to leave our sheep back in Virginia.

Suk asked us to leave the card with her. She said, "I would like to paint this, and if it turns out right I will give it to you; if not, I won't mention it again." In a couple of weeks, there she was waiting for us, with a gift of a beautiful painting. To us it looks like one of the Old Masters. It brings us joy whenever we look at it and when we explain to guests how it came to be.

Suk and her husband Wes have become our good friends. We have learned that Suk's family in Korea had orchards of all kinds—apples and peaches, like my family in Virginia, as well as many other kinds of fruit. We learned that when Suk paints sheep, she usually paints eight in the picture, because she comes from a family of eight, and the sheep represent her family.

Sometimes when we are asked why we accepted interim pastorates, we have a hard time explaining. But we know that each time we accepted another pastoral role, we gained new experiences and met new friends that would not otherwise have come to us.

We are so thankful for the friendship of Dorothy and her family, and of Suk and Wes and so many others we met in and around Lancaster, Pennsylvania. Our sheep pictures are a constant reminder of these rich experiences.

4

The Meanest Service

She was the only person who looked at me and listened to me!

We were taking a tour of the church of our new assignment. It was a ten-year-old church, and it was in impeccable condition! We commented on this to our guide, and she replied that all the cleaning and upkeep of the church was done by volunteers.

Especially the women's bathroom was everything you could hope for. Betty asked the guide, "But how does anybody keep a room this spotless?" Our guide replied that one woman in the church specifically asked for the women's restroom assignment and that she takes special pride in keeping it "just so."

When we came away from the church after that first introduction, the cleanliness was the main impression that stayed with us. Somehow it said good things about the people there.

In his book *Life Together*, Dietrich Bonhoeffer makes a profound statement: "Nobody is too good for the meanest service." Many voices call us to upward mobility. But in Christ's own teaching, "Those who love their life lose it, and those who hate their life in this world will keep it for eternal life" (John 12:25). And in Philippians 2, we read that Jesus himself took on the form of a slave.

I once read about a large medical center that surveyed all the patients who had entered their hospital in the previous year. The survey asked:
- What was the most helpful service provided?
- What made you feel cared for?
- What made you feel comfortable and at ease?
- What helped most during your illness?

Many of the answers were predictable. Some mentioned a doctor, a surgeon, a nurse, an administrator, a chaplain. But over and over, patients mentioned a woman named Edna.

Edna, the woman with the mop
  Who waxed the floor,
    Dusted the furniture,
      Cleaned up the messes.

One man wrote in his survey that he had undergone major surgery. He reported that when his pain medication wore off in the middle of the night the pain surged, so he tried to get help. "I pressed the 'Call' button again and again," he said.

But nobody responded to the call button, apparently because, the man speculated, all the nurses were too busy.

Then something different happened. A woman with a mop appeared. She asked, "Honey, are you all right?"

No! He most definitely wasn't.

Edna gave him her full attention; she looked into his eyes. The patient believed she was the only one who really looked at and listened to him. He remembered that everyone else came into the room in a hurry, stuck a thermometer in his mouth, checked blood pressure, filled out the chart, and left.

Only Edna gave undivided attention. She listened. She connected with him. Only Edna!

Philippians 2:5-7. Let the same mind be in you that was in Christ Jesus, who, though he was in the form of God, did not regard equality with God as something to be exploited, but emptied himself, taking the form of a slave.

5

A Trip to Remember

We squeezed through a tight stairway to a high tower to see one more place of agony.

In 2006 we signed up for an Anabaptist Heritage Tour. This is something we had often talked about doing, but we never seemed to have the necessary two-week opening in our schedules. Finally the time was right and we were determined to accomplish this lifelong dream.

Several close friends and relatives also expressed interest. Betty's sister, Louretta Wilson, and my cousins Rowland and Thelma Shank as well as our friend Christine Hill decided to go. We knew we would have more fun if family and friends shared the journey. All together, forty "tourists" would take this memorable trip together.

The brochure said we would visit seven countries in Europe's heartland: Holland, Belgium, France, Germany, Austria, Liechtenstein, and Switzerland. The promotional flyer described some of the highlights. We would:
- visit ancient cathedrals and castles and art museums,
- take a cruise on the Rhine,
- explore the famous Alkmaar Cheese Market in Amsterdam, and
- cross the dike at the Zuiderzee.

All these things we had heard about from traveling friends, and we were eager for the experience. So we called for reservations and started the process of updating passports in preparation for the trip of a lifetime.

Our tour leaders were Myron and Esther Augsburger. Myron, a devoted student of Anabaptist history, would share his expertise. And Esther with her high interest and experience as an artist and sculptor would enrich our understandings. Dave and Joyce Eshleman were the coordinators.

It looked like a full schedule, and we were ready for adventure. Several days into the trip we remembered that the brochure had mentioned "leisure time" but we soon learned that with Myron there's not much of that.

We learned many details about our painful history as Anabaptist Christians. We walked beside the river where executions by drowning took place.

We stood in parks, and read the plaques describing where martyrs were burned at the stake.

We climbed high towers where martyrs were held for execution. We sang praises to the "God from whom all blessings flow," a favorite song of many Mennonites (sometimes known as "606" based on its location in one hymnbook) in the music room of King Ludwig's Castle. Our tour guide responded as though she had never heard anything so beautiful.

We visited a torture chamber where we could see many grotesque tools that were used to inflict pain.

We climbed the hill to experience a worship service in the legendary "Anabaptist Cave" where early Mennonites worshiped during times of persecution. (The climb to the cave was made more difficult by a light drizzle and slippery rocks. That night Betty wrote in her journal, "Way too much walking! We put this trip off until it was almost too late! We are among the oldest in the group.")

We visited the infamous Dachau concentration camp of World War II. Our group joined thousands of other tourists walking through the gates, and we were moved to tears as we remembered the grisly history of this place.

Sometimes we thought we'd had enough of martyrs. We appreciated the history, but we were tired of thinking about it.

When we traveled near Augsburg, Germany, we kidded Myron about stopping the bus so we could buy Augsburger beer!

On our final day in Switzerland, in Emmental, we realized that we were driving by the place where Emmental cheese (the one with the holes) originates. We had heard of this Mennonite cheese maker and had hoped to take a block of cheese along home.

But I heard Myron reply to somebody's request, "There is one more martyr site I want you to visit. It's the Trachselwald Castle. Here you must see where countless Anabaptists were chained in wooden cells. You will see the imprint of their heads where they lay down to sleep."

So on that final day, we reluctantly followed our leader, squeezing through the tight little stairway to the attic of a high tower to see one more place of agony.

When the trip was ended we were welcomed at Dulles Airport by the bus driver from Harrisonburg, Virginia. From Harrisonburg we went our separate ways to our homes in Ohio, Oregon, New Jersey, Indiana, Illinois, Iowa, Maryland, North Carolina, and Virginia. We gave thanks for our safe arrival home.

But we did not have cheese from the Mennonite cheese maker in Emmental! What we did have was a treasure of memories that will last a lifetime and a new appreciation for all those Anabaptist mothers and fathers who went before, paving the way despite severe persecution, building our rich heritage.

6

Renewal Through Baptism

A line began to form.
Nearly one hundred people came forward.

For the ten-month period after I had finished writing *That Amazing Junk-Man* and it was in the hands of the publisher, I was interim pastor at Neffsville Mennonite Church in Pennsylvania. Each week as I prepared the upcoming sermon, a story from the book would come to mind. I found that by reading aloud to the congregation in the first minutes of the sermon, I could capture the attention of young and old alike. First the story, then the sermon.

One Sunday three young people were to be baptized. All week I had been remembering the story about my friend Roy a few years earlier. Roy had been touched and warmed by his granddaughters' baptism. He said, "It's been so long since my own baptism, I sometimes believe I should be baptized again." And one morning, in the middle of the week, in a quiet office in the church, Roy was rebaptized. All of us in the room had felt our own souls refreshed.

Every church has persons like Roy who have followed Jesus for a long time. As new Christians we were energetic and we tried to walk closely in his steps. Over time we may lose that sense of immediacy and we may follow at a distance. We need new signs, some fresh reminders, to stay close to our Master.

So I read the story of Roy, entitled "A New Beginning," and followed with the morning text and a brief sermon. Then I suggested to the congregation, "Perhaps there are some present this morning who, like Roy, are saying to yourselves, 'The way has been long. I can barely remember my own baptism. I would like to receive the fresh wind of the Spirit.'"

We proceeded with the baptism of the three young people. Then the invitation was open for anyone who would like to experience anew their first baptism. The associate pastor was prepared to help, and I asked to be the first to receive this second baptism. We waited a few minutes and one or two stepped forward. Then a line began to form. Nearly a hundred people came to experience this rebaptism.

At age seventy-four I received my second baptism. It had been sixty-three years since my first baptism, when I was eleven years old. Thank God for times of renewal and new life in the Spirit.

> *Matthew 3:16-17.* At that moment heaven was opened, and [Jesus] saw the Spirit of God descending like a dove and lighting on him. And a voice from heaven said, "This is my Son, whom I love; with him I am well pleased."

7

A Note from the Other Side

*Ethel lay down to rest,
went to sleep, and never woke up.*

This beautiful card I hold in my hand is not really from heaven. But it came to me after the passing of a dear friend, and so it seemed like it was her final message that found its way to earth from the other side.

During our brief interim ministry at Landisville Mennonite Church in Pennsylvania, we came to love and appreciate Arthur and Ethel Miller. Arthur had retired from the ministry at Landisville twenty years before our coming to the church. Ethel had been the loyal and respected wife of the minister. Both of them continued long after retirement to make their contributions in so many ways.

Arthur and Ethel were also founders of Miller's Greenhouse, less than a mile from the church. Their children and grandchildren now manage the thriving business. During the congregation's early years, before Mennonite ministers were paid, the greenhouse income provided for their large family.

Whenever we visited the Millers, we learned more about the early years of the church and grew in our respect for the groundwork laid by these two saints. Both of the Millers were in their nineties and needing more and more support from family and friends. Their children stopped in often, prepared meals for them, and in numerous ways gave assistance so they could remain in their own home.

One afternoon Ethel went to her room to rest, and this is where she was found by her husband. She just went to sleep and never woke up. We were able to attend the funeral and once again see the family's loving care as they planned her beautiful memorial service.

Several weeks after her death, at church one Sunday morning Arthur handed me an envelope. "Ethel was writing this for you and she would want me to see that you get it," he said.

We opened the envelope to find a beautiful, delicate card. It is a reproduction from an original painting by artist Phyllis Leonetti. Inside, in Ethel's shaky handwriting, is this note:

Dear Truman and Betty,
  There is a saying that—
"The Seventies Are the Youth of Old Age."

We wish for you the Joy of Youth
  And the Privileges of Old Age.
    —Arthur and Ethel Miller, in the Nineties

How profound is that? We felt joyful and youthful because of this blessing from somebody twenty years older, and from one now graduated to the other side!

8

Symbolic Gifts

Here I am sitting on my big leather sofa, watching the snow.

The north wind doth blow
And we shall have snow
And what will the robin do then, oh then?
He'll fly to the barn
and keep himself warm.
—From "Mother Goose"

    Today is the first snowfall of the year. The Weather Channel predicted this snow, but I didn't pay much attention. I don't have to get up early or stay up late to hear which schools are closed and which church services have been canceled.

    Retirement seems to be all about having time. Here I am sitting on my big leather sofa, watching the snow and having time to reflect. On my lap is a soft, furry Alpaca blanket that was given to us when we left the Neffsville church. I feel the warmth of the blanket and remember the warmth of the Neffsville folks.

    Just outside the living room window are the chimes that play when the wind blows. The chimes were a gift from Landisville, Pennsylvania, at the end of our interim service there. They were presented to us at the end of Gina's children's story.

Gina talked with the children about the wind of the Spirit and she held the gift up so that the chimes rang. She expressed the hope that when the chimes ring in Virginia we will think of the church family there at Landisville. And that is exactly what happens. The chimes ring and we remember.

Under the big dogwood tree in our front yard, just eight feet away from the chimes, stands a rustic plank, with hand-carved letters, "PEACE ON EARTH." This was a gift from Ben and Bertha Brubaker, members at Landisville.

A warm blanket, soft music, and peace on earth. All of these are wonderful symbols of the warmth and music and friendships in those northern places. How blessed can a person be?

9

Agape Class Retreat

*God's presence invaded
our space in a fresh way.*

While we worked and lived for eighteen years in Pennsylvania, we knew that in our retirement years we would return to the Shenandoah Valley of Virginia. Both of our children considered the Valley as "home," and we felt the same way.

We made the move to Virginia and settled into a more leisurely pace. I worked half-time in a pastoral role at a local church. We joined the Agape Sunday school class and developed a new set of friends.

Soon after joining the class, Betty and I were asked to lead Agape's annual retreat. In choosing a theme for the weekend—maybe to meet our own needs–we considered non-threatening ways class members could learn to know each other better. We recognized that our class, like many Sunday school classes, might meet every Sunday for years and remain strangers to each other.

At the time I was reading the book, *Sacred Stories*, edited by Charles and Anne Simpkinson (HarperSan Francisco, 1993). I was intrigued by the idea that our personal stories tell us about ourselves and at the same time connect us with our fellow human beings.

We decided that storytelling would be our theme for the weekend. We received a go-ahead from the class leaders. Each member would bring to the retreat one story about one happening in his or her life. They could bring an "artifact" along if it would help tell the story.

Throughout the retreat weekend we read snatches aloud from *Sacred Stories*. One passage described the Dogon culture in Africa and their emphasis on storytelling. For the Dogon, the true word is spoken sitting down. "The word spoken sitting down is thoughtful speech. The word spoken while walking is speech without position and therefore forgotten" (p. 159).

A big, comfortable rocking chair was brought into the circle. As participants prepared for their turn, they would settle into the rocking chair and receive our full attention.

Lorraine brought a battered suitcase and told a story of the many moves her family made during her school years—ten moves in twelve years. Miriam showed a tiny formal dress that fit her when she was eight years old. Super-musician that she is, already she was playing for weddings at an early age.

When it was Sam's turn to tell a story, he held in his hands a toy sand-loader. His father had received it as a special gift when he was hospitalized, at age nine, in 1926. With much cranking and turning, Sam patiently demonstrated how "Sandy Andy" carries a load of sand and moves it from this place to that place. Sam became a child again, experiencing the laughter and love and fun of a young boy at home. It was a fresh insight for me to see this accomplished medical doctor in this relaxed state.

What a great way to enjoy a glimpse into each other's lives. It was a weekend of feeling like family together. God's presence invaded our space in a fresh way. We understood a little more the meaning of our name, Agape, God's love for us.

10

The Storms of Life

*For years George remembered
that terrible day.*

George and Lei Wong have been our dear friends for more than forty years. When we moved to the Shenandoah Valley, our backyards joined. Their two little ones, Lisa and Michael, were the same ages as our Kathleen and Don. Then their third child, Sammy, was born. We have a huge store of memories from those years when the children were small.

George grew up in mainland China. The year he turned fourteen, his mother decided that George should go to live for awhile with his uncle and aunt in Hawaii. He would help his uncle in the family grocery store near Hilo Bay.

Every morning George helped his uncle open the store, then walked to school for the day. One morning when he and his uncle came to work, they found the store had been flooded. They did not realize that a tsunami was in progress and that the first wave had hit that morning.

George was told to go on to school while his uncle cleaned up the mess. George left the building, heading for school. Suddenly he heard someone cry out, "Run! Run! Big wave coming in!" George looked up to see a mountainous wave headed toward him.

The wave kept coming. People were covered up with the wave. Some were washed out to sea, and many drowned. George ran for all he was worth, almost bumping into a photographer taking a picture of the surging water.

For years George remembered that terrible day when the tsunami hit the shores of Hilo Bay and people died trying to escape. He tried to describe to Lei the awful wave that nearly overtook him. He always added, "I almost bumped into a man taking pictures."

Then in 1998, George and Lei were watching a television documentary on "Great Storms of the Twentieth Century." Lei half-joking said, "Let's watch this! We might see a picture of you." All at once George did see himself in the picture, the fourteen-year-old boy fleeing in front of the massive wave. "That's me!" he cried out. His picture had been captured by the cameraman he almost ran over.

A few years later George and Lei with their children and grandchildren visited the Pacific Tsunami Museum in Hilo, Hawaii. They saw the huge mural in the entrance to the museum, the very same picture in the documentary.

A family member told the museum staff that George, who was standing there, was that fourteen-year-old boy. The director of the museum later wrote, "This answered the fifty-five-year-old question, 'Who is the boy in the picture?'"

I have a copy of this famous photograph, called the "Signature Picture" of the April 1, 1946, tsunami in Hilo Bay, Hawaii. It serves as a reminder of how fragile and precious life is and how much I value the friendship of that boy who outran the tsunami.

11

How Many Pastors Does It Take?

It finally dawned on me that Akron was actually three churches.

One night last month, Don Gunden called the house. He and Elsie were traveling through Harrisonburg on I-81 South, had settled into a motel for the night, and hoped we could meet them for breakfast.

Don and Elsie are good friends from Pennsylvania. Don believes in keeping in touch and goes out of his way to make sure it happens. It has been twenty-five years since we lived and worked in the same area. But when we get together it seems like we can make instant connections.

We first learned to know Don when we received the call from Akron, Pennsylvania, to consider coming as pastor. Don was on the search committee and evidently appointed by the committee to be the contact person. From the beginning, he gave us hints as to how we should interact with this "northern" church.

Until that time, we had always used professional movers when we transferred to a new location. But the move from Virginia to Pennsylvania was going to be more expensive than usual, and the church would be paying the bill. Don said it would look good to the congregation if we rented a U-Haul.

We followed his suggestion. We had professional movers load the U-Haul for us, and, sure enough, there were plenty of church people at the other end to unload the furniture and place it in our new home. If I recall correctly, they made a party out of the occasion, with food and fellowship.

Don had other helpful suggestions. We understood that he was on the inside track, that he knew how people were thinking, and that we were pretty safe if we checked things out with him. He was also a generous parishioner. I remember opening the door at Christmastime when he delivered the biggest poinsettia I had ever seen.

Don was more than a member of the church. I started to think of him as one of the "unofficial pastors" at Akron. It had finally dawned on me that Akron Mennonite Church was actually three churches: the MCC (Mennonite Central Committee) families with their emphasis on simple living; the business people who drove nice cars and lived in lovely homes; and the jet set who took jaunts to New York City and played golf and tennis.

It seemed to me that each group had its pastor and if I stayed in close touch with these key people, they could help keep the church running smoothly. In my mind, Don was the pastor of the business group. When there was an issue with this third of the church, I could discuss it with Don and he would be the facilitator or mediator as needed. It worked the same for the other two groups. I may have been the official pastor, but I knew who the real movers and shakers were.

This was a helpful insight. In fact, at every church I have served, I have learned to look for the key people who serve in this capacity. It has been a blessing and a privilege to share the burden of ministry with these unofficial pastors.

12

Interim Pastors, Temporary Shepherds

The elders offered to sit with us around our dining room table.

What do interim pastors know? Often in the prior two years we had found ourselves in the obvious situation of "not knowing" what everybody else in the congregation already knew. All we could do was laugh and say, "What do interim pastors know?"

The thought of being an interim pastor had never entered my mind. In the fall of 2006 I was happily transitioning into retirement, finishing the book I had been waiting so long to write.

When the phone rang, I heard someone saying they were calling on behalf of Neffsville Mennonite Church in Lancaster, Pennsylvania. The Neffsville pastor had just resigned after a short term as lead pastor. The church needed an interim pastor to hold things together until a new pastor could be found.

Right away I was intrigued. I knew and admired the young pastor when he was a seminary student. My initial thought was, *I can go to Neffsville and help him through whatever rough spots he is experiencing, and talk him out of resigning.*

That's not how it worked out. The pastor had made up his mind. He loved the church. In fact, he wanted to remain a member of the church, but he did not want to be the pastor. He insisted to the elders that there were no church problems or difficulties; he just wanted out of the pastor's role.

So the overseer was calling to find out if I was interested and I said, "Yes." Betty and I drove to Neffsville, met with some of the elders, and returned home after the interview. Within the week, they called and said they had decided to ask a local person to be their interim pastor. It would simplify everything. The person would not have to uproot himself as I would need to do.

It made sense. I thanked them for thinking of me in the first place, put the file away, and forgot about the whole thing. But in two weeks, another call came. This time it was the lead elder. He said, "We have egg on our face. We presented our candidate to the congregation and they turned him down. Will you reconsider our invitation?"

We needed a couple of days to think about this. When I returned the call to the elder, I said: "I will consider your invitation under two conditions: One, that there are no other candidates, and two, that Betty will be hired as associate interim pastor." Soon the call came back. Both conditions were accepted, and the four elders offered to come to Virginia to meet with us around our dining room table.

We asked clear questions: Are there any unresolved issues? Any problems? Does anybody really know the reason the pastor is leaving? No, they were quick to answer, No problems, a happy working team.

Before the elders left that day, we said we would commit for up to one year. They would take our names to the congregation. We drove to Neffsville for a Sunday morning of interaction with the congregation. The vote was affirmative.

We would need a place in Lancaster to live. We found a small, one-bedroom apartment that met our budget and our needs. We packed our bags and a few belongings. By November 1 Betty and I were installed as interim pastor and associate pastor at Neffsville.

In the few weeks before the move, we tried to think how to prepare for this new assignment. We bought a book written by Alan G. Gripe, *The Interim Pastor's Manual*. We read how interim pastors need to provide a "non-anxious presence" when a church is naturally in an anxious state.

We called Laban Peachey who has been interim pastor in eight or ten different churches. Laban's advice was helpful. He said, "You love the people, and you don't get involved with any of their issues."

Love the people. It was easy to do. They were grieving their loss of a pastor. They were eager to get back on track. There were issues of self-esteem, wondering what they might have done to cause the pastor to leave.

The search committee continued the quest for a new pastor. Over several months they read many profiles of possible candidates and narrowed the search to a young couple from our home church in Virginia.

We knew this couple, Harry and Beth Jarrett, and we were thrilled to learn of the possibility. It was a great pleasure to encourage and support them as they made their move to the community and took up the pastoral duties. Later we heard good reports of their ministry.

13

Hello and Good-bye

*The spotless bathrooms
made a huge impression on us.*

The people at Neffsville Mennonite Church in Pennsylvania became very dear to Betty and me. A special bond developed that we can't quite explain. But no matter how much we loved church and people, we were eager to be back home.

I started hearing Betty say, "This is a once-in-a-lifetime experience. It's been good, but never again." The whole scene of moving, living in a little apartment, missing our own home and our view of the West Virginia mountains—all these contributed to our eagerness to return home.

By September 2007, we were home again, trying to catch up with a neglected yard and garden and basement. We settled in and enjoyed the Thanksgiving and Christmas seasons at home. We enjoyed being in our own Sunday school class (Agape) at Harrisonburg Mennonite Church.

But in a few weeks we received another phone call, this time from Dale Stoltzfus, representing the Landisville Mennonite Church also in Pennsylvania. He asked if we would be interested in another interim ministry for six months or so.

I told Dale we would think about it and pray, and that he should call back in a week. During that week, we made plans to say a polite No. When Dale called again, Betty answered the phone and was reaching to hand it over to me when Dale said, "No, I want to talk to you!" He asked Betty to serve as associate interim pastor along with me in the pastor role.

Betty is a trained and experienced social worker. She loves her work and has never thought of herself as a pastor. Now she says it was an ego trip to be asked to become an associate interim pastor!

We traveled to Landisville and met with their committees. We saw the clean, clean church, the spotless bathrooms, and learned that *all* the church cleaning is done by member-volunteers. This made a huge impression. This was another group of people who love their church. Why would we *not* want to come and serve for a few months?

There was a strong pastoral team in place, with well-functioning committees. We discovered there would be a comfortable, affordable place to stay, in the *Dawdyhaus* extension of Dr. Clarence and Helen Rutt's residence.

We did not know how to explain this change in plans to our Agape Sunday school class. During prayer and praise time Betty told the class of our new assignment. She tried to explain, "We want to do this, and we don't want to do this."

The teacher that morning was Jim Kidd, and he said we reminded him of a story: Parents took their young son to a psychologist to figure out what was wrong with him. The psychologist gave them a diagnosis: "Pyromania with feeling of ambivalence." The parents asked what that meant, and the counselor replied: "He keeps setting the fire and then stomps it out, then sets it again and stomps it out."

By February 1, 2007, we were installed in the pastoral office vacated by Sam Thomas who had been the beloved pastor at Landisville for eighteen years. Again, what a loving and supportive church family we found. We were there for seven months, gained the ten pounds we had just lost, and celebrated when the church found their new pastor, Randall Shull.

14

Read the Manual

*Many churches try to get by
without hiring an interim pastor.*

While we were still occupying the pastor's office at Landisville Mennonite Church in Pennsylvania the phone rang. A stranger on the other end said, "Your name has been given to us as a possible interim pastor for our church. Would you be interested in coming to help us for a year?"

I replied, "I am seventy-five!" The person said, "Oh!" and after some polite chitchat the conversation was over.

In another week there was another phone call. This time when asked the question, I had to say, "I am seventy-six." Again the person said, "Oh!" That was the end of the conversation.

It is time for us to settle down and reconnect with our old friends in our own neighborhood. We need to eat in our own home and stop eating in restaurants. We need to go to the gym and use the exercise machines. We need to sign up for water aerobics and get serious about our own health.

But what a rich and rewarding experience to have served those months in the interim role at Landisville and elsewhere. As always, we learned as we went along and wish we had known then what we know now.

We learned that a church in crisis is like a family in crisis.

While members experience grief or anxiety, they are open to suggestions and possible changes. One of "our churches" was in a more anxious state. They were also the most open to our suggestions.

In *The Interim Pastor's Manual*, Alan G. Gripe explains that many churches try to get by without hiring an interim pastor and that these churches are asking for trouble. In the vacuum left by the departing pastor, current staff members sometimes reach out and extend themselves beyond their assigned duties. Then have difficulty letting go when the new pastor arrives.

In one of "our churches," this is exactly what had happened before they hired their young pastor who had soon resigned. Staff had stepped in and then found it difficult to give the new pastor room to carry out the duties of the lead pastoral role.

At both of the churches the pastoral teams were easy to work with. They were open to suggestions that had been useful to me in other churches. Three things in particular worked well in the interim situation.

1. Working with the team, we established an overall theme that seemed especially appropriate for a church "in between pastors." The theme originates in a series by Richard C. Meyer, called One Anothering. Among others, the topics in this series include these:
- Love One Another
- Care for One Another
- Encourage and Build Up One Another
- Pray for One Another
- Admonish One Another

I highly recommend such a series for interim teams. It provides a way to focus on the strengths and needs of a congregation. Different members of the team were asked to preach on their choice of these subjects.

2. We initiated a monthly thank offering (celebrating birthdays and anniversaries and other happy occasions) for building up the compassion fund. This offering is different from the regular Sunday offerings. For the Thank Offering, we asked the musicians to step up the tempo while men, women, and children "danced" to the front to place a love offering in the basket.

3. "Coffee with a Pastor" is one of the most rewarding projects I have enjoyed in all my church work. Individuals and couples would come to have an hour alone with a pastor. They could use the time in whatever way they chose: to discuss family and personal history, work problems, church issues, or anything at all.

Especially in an interim period, where the pastor is in a hurry to learn to know the church family, this coffee hour is helpful. The hour of conversation revealed the pain and grief that members were experiencing, either in their own families or as a member of the church family.

There was the normal grief of losing a beloved pastor. There were expressions of feeling outside the loop in the life of the church. Some family crises needed outside support. Financial struggles sometimes could be alleviated with the growing Compassion Fund.

We were greatly enriched when the people accepted this invitation to come and meet with team members. Betty and I think we had individual sessions with at least seventy-five people at each of the churches. It was a privilege to join the church family in this way. If anyone should ask us what we learned about being interim pastors, the above ideas are some of the things we would suggest.

Through it all, when we caught ourselves feeling anxious, we remembered the advice that the interim pastor is to be "a non-anxious presence" in a time of some anxiety.

15

Bless One Another (*Sermon*)

Bishop John E. Lapp said,
"I must bless my children before I die."

Text: Numbers 6:24-27

People come to church for a whole variety of reasons. First of all, it is hoped, we come to receive heavenly food, to be nourished in our faith, and to renew our covenants with God and his people. We also come to be affirmed and loved by spiritual brothers and sisters and fathers and mothers.

Henri Nouwen was on the faculty at Yale, then at Harvard, for many years. About those years, Henri writes, "My whole life I had been surrounded by well-meaning encouragement to go 'higher up.' Folks would say to me, 'You can do so much good there, for so many people.'" But Nouwen explains that he left Yale and Harvard feeling impoverished in his soul and went to serve at L'Arche Community in Toronto, a community of broken people.

He was responsible there to care for one severely handicapped man who could not take care of his personal needs,

or walk one step without help,
    could not put food into his own mouth,
        and could not speak a word.

While taking care of Adam,
    Nouwen found renewal.
        He discovered a way
            to joy and peace
                and soul satisfaction.

In the book, Life of the Beloved, *Nouwen*
describes some of the residents attending a Sunday evening vespers
    at L'Arche.
As Nouwen entered the room,
    a young woman named Janet
        came to him before the service saying,
            "Henri, I need a blessing."

Nouwen reached out to Janet,
    to make the sign of the cross
        on her forehead
            (a priestly gesture),

but Janet drew back.
    "No, no. I mean a real blessing."
So Henri, in his priestly robes,
    opened wide his arms,
        wrapped them around Janet, and said,

"Janet, you are God's beloved daughter.
    God loves you and we love you.
        Your beautiful smile,
        your kind spirit,
        all the kind things you do for us,
            you are loved by all of us.
        "I want you to remember who you are.
    You are a child of God
        And loved by all the people here with you."

Janet raised her head.
    Her broad smile
        showed that a transformation had happened.
            The community's response was immediate and electric!
A young man raised his hand and said,
"What about me? I need a blessing!"
    Nouwen said, "Come!"
He wrapped his arms around John and said,
    "John, it is good you are here,
    you are God's beloved child."

One by one, the members of the community came
    seeking a blessing,
until all the residents had been blessed.

There was a pause,
    then one of the staff members raised his hand,
"Henri, I need a blessing."
And it started all over again.

Like Janet, don't we often feel
    we have missed the blessing?
Like Janet, we might hear an inner voice calling us
    worthless, useless,
        evil, bad, rotten,
            doomed to darkness and death.

When we gather to worship and adore our God,
    it may seem that we are strong
        and have it all together.
But all of us are broken people.
    We come together to seek God's blessing.
We come seeking the blessing of our brothers and sisters.
We come to hear that we are God's children.

The Bible is a book of blessing.
    In the FIRST chapter
        of the FIRST book of the Bible,
we read words of blessing:

*"God blessed Adam and Eve and said to them,
'Be fruitful and increase in number;
  fill the earth and subdue it.'"—Genesis 1:28*

*In the LAST chapter of the LAST book of the Bible,
  we again read words of blessing:*

*"Blessed are those who wash their robes,
  that they may have the right to the
    tree of life
and may go through the gates
  into the city."—Revelation 22:14*

*In Numbers 6:24-26 we find a
  universal blessing
    meant for every human being:*

*"The Lord bless you and keep you;
the Lord make his face shine upon you
  and be gracious to you;
the Lord turn his face toward you
  and give you peace."*

*I notice in the Gospels that Jesus reaches out
to the "un-blessed":
  Healing a demon-possessed man,
    the Cyrophoenician woman,
    a deaf and mute man,
    a blind man.
We read the stories of Jesus,
  always moving down, down, down
    to the lower place of service,
  to the damaged and wounded people:
No hand touched theirs,
  Never a kiss on their cheek,
    No one said," I love you,"
      No one gazed into their eyes,
        No one listened to their story,
        No one cared.*

*Our society, too, is severely under-blessed.
Our church is under-blessed.*

*We too live in a broken, torn, and sinful world.
Look at the torture, the killings,
    the destruction of cities,
        the spoiling of nature.
Can we extend blessing in such a setting?*

*I remember Bishop John E. Lapp.
    Brother Lapp was a saintly man
        who lived in eastern Pennsylvania.
As an old man he thought about giving a blessing
    to each of his children.
He said, "I must bless my children before I die!"*

*He wrote out a blessing for each of his nine children:
one the director of MCC (Mennonite Central Committee),
    a college president,
        several ministers,
            teachers and counselors,
                authors,
                    some working in business.*

*A blessing was written for each child.
    Then he made reservations
at Spruce Lake Retreat Center
    and brought the family together.
He read his blessing to each child.
    The whole family was blessed!*

*Every congregation has people who are
    lonely, unloved,
        unaffirmed, never touched.
God's people need each other!
    We might even need to hear,
"You are looking especially lovely today!"*

*Wouldn't God want us to speak well of God's creation?
Can we do this for each other in the family of God?*

We are all called to bless and be blessed.
    Have you heard the words,
        "You are a child of God.
            God is pleased with you."
Have you given this gift to others
    (at home, at work, in the church)?
The power that we possess
    is awesome.

Savor again the profound blessing from Numbers 6:24-26:
"The Lord bless you and keep you;
the Lord make his face shine upon you
    and be gracious to you;
the Lord turn his face toward you
    and give you peace."

Amen.

16

Confess Your Sins One to Another (*Sermon*)

Nearly all of us are broken, wounded people.

Text: James 5:13-20

Many of you have read Richard Foster's book, *Celebration of Discipline: The Path to Spiritual Growth,* in which he describes the disciplines of prayer and fasting, meditation, confession, and emphasizes these are to be celebrated. By practicing these disciplines, we mature in our Christian spirituality and abundant life.

In one chapter, tucked in near the end of the book, Foster lets us in on a very personal story:

He longed for some power to do the work of God.
He prayed, "Lord, is there more you want to bring into my life? If something is blocking the flow of your power, reveal it to me."
He devised a plan to divide his life into three segments:
    Childhood years,
      Adolescent years,
        Adult years.

He invited God to reveal anything
    in each of these stages,
        that needed forgiveness
            or healing
                or both.
He waited in absolute silence for a time,
    before writing down what came to mind.
Then, paper in hand,
    he went to a dear brother in Christ
        and asked him to hear his confession.
Carefully Foster read the lists,
    all these "sins" or "weaknesses"
        that he could remember.
When he finished, he started to return the paper to his briefcase.
The friend intervened. Foster writes,
"I watched him tear the paper
    into tiny pieces
        and drop them into the wastebasket.
I knew then that my sins had been removed
as far as the east is from the west."

The friend prayed a prayer of healing
    for all the sorrows and hurts of Richard's past.

Foster notes an interesting sidelight:
    This exposure of his humanity
        apparently sparked
            a freedom in his counselor-friend.
For directly following his prayer for Foster,
    the friend was able to express a deep, troubling sin
        that until then he had been unable to confess.

Several things stand out in this story:

Nearly all of us are broken, wounded people.
    We have all sinned and come short of God's glory.
        If you are a student of the Bible,
        you will recognize that the spiritual giants
            we admire

at some time were fallen giants.
(Moses, David, Solomon, Paul)
We need to learn all over again
    the meaning of being a spiritual family:
        brothers and sisters who love one another,
            Pray for one another,
        Care for one another.
        Bear one another's burdens,
      Encourage one another,
    Submit to one another,
Admonish one another.

We cannot be Christian alone.
    We need each other.
Women may be better at this than men.
    Women admit they need other women
        to share their everyday hopes and dreams,
            to share their disappointments and grief.
We read that only ten percent of men have someone
    they can call a close, real friend.
Men tend to keep their thoughts and feelings to themselves.
    "People might use my weaknesses to take advantage of me."
    "If they really know me, they will think less of me."

Whether man or woman, we need to cultivate the idea of
    "One-anothering"
        in which we develop our concept of
            mercy, forgiveness, and healing.
God is a God of second chances.
    God allows us to begin again.
        God believes in forgiveness,
            and healing, and new beginnings.

Ponder the profound promises in Psalm 103:
"Who forgives all your sins,
    and heals all your diseases,
        who redeems your life from the pit,
            and crowns you with love and compassion."

"The Lord is compassionate and gracious,
    slow to anger, abounding in love.
        He will not always accuse,
            nor will he harbor his anger forever.
"He does not treat us as our sins deserve
    or repay us according to our iniquities.
        For as high as the heavens are above the earth,
            so great is his love
                for those who fear him.
        As far as the east is from the west,
            so far has he removed our transgressions from us."

The Bible says we are all sinners in need of forgiveness.
God forgives.
God not only forgives,
    God also forgets.
What does it mean
that God blots out our transgressions?
What it means is that
we can begin with a clean slate.
    We are made new in Christ.
        Creatures made new!
We can come out of the woods
        Cleaned,
        Renewed,
                Our slate clean!
We experience joy and peace,
filled with power from God (Rom. 4:8).

God does not count our sin against us.
    We incur debt, but
        God puts nothing in the debit column.
    We owe,
        but we don't have to pay.
    God puts our wrongdoing behind his back (Isa. 38:17).
        God looks at us but does not see our wrongdoing.
    God blots out our sin (Isa. 43:25).

We have spilled indelible ink on our new outfit,
    but God makes the stain disappear.

With God there are no unforgivable sins.
    This is hard for us humans to accept.
        How do we handle a God who
            forgives and forgives and forgives?

I have a friend,
    a divorced woman.
        Sitting in church one day,
            she saw her former husband,
                with a new woman on his arm,
                      approaching the communion table.
    "How dare God forgive such a scoundrel?"

We live in a world of injustice
    and murder,
        villages burned,
            women raped,
                fathers with slit throats.

We ask,
How dare God forgive?

God's forgiveness is a gift.

    Not one of us deserves such a gift.
        We cannot earn it.
            It is pure gift.
    Do we know what we are singing when we celebrate the
        "Marvelous grace of our loving Lord"
    whose blood was poured out on Calvary for us?

    God forgives; we too need to forgive.
        Is it possible for us, mere humans,
            to forgive the way we should?
    If God is our model,
        We must have love,
        We must have mercy.
        We must blur the memory of the wrong.

We acknowledge that our forgiving is faulty.
   God's is faultless.
Our forgiving is provisional.
   God's is final.
We forgive hesitantly.
   God forgives without hesitation.

We must, like God,
   forgive and forget.
How hard it is!
We like to give partial forgiveness,
   hold back some weapon for later use.
     We find it hard to wipe the slate clean.

How many times do I forgive with my mouth
   but hold resentment in my heart?
We keep a low-grade hostility
   toward those we have "forgiven"
     but really have not forgiven.

God asks us to be forgiving, kind, generous.

I need to own that,
   for me and for my church,
there is no future without forgiveness.

What might "Forgiveness Sunday" look like in my church?
   Who am I having problems with?
Where do I hold a grudge
   that I am not willing to let go?
What would it mean for me to say,
   as God says,
"There are no unforgivable sins."

   We need to confess,
     forgive,
        show mercy and kindness.
We celebrate our spiritual family,
   and we build each other up.

17

Wash One Another's Feet (*Sermon*)

*The world does not
begin to understand this concept.*

Text: John 13:1-17

The Gospel of John can be understood
    as Jesus' farewell address.
Soon he will be leaving the earth,
    and he wants to give some final instructions
        to his disciples.

The book of John provides important clues
    and warnings
about the "big world"
    and the tiny little band of disciples,
        the first church.
The world is big and the church is small.

Jesus describes the world as destructive,
    with demonic energies on the loose,
        creating chaos.
We are foolish if we do not see
    the destructive forces around us:

9/11 is etched in our minds,
   tsunami images, hurricanes, and earthquakes,
      Iraq—the unthinkable, terrible death toll;
         AIDS epidemics—out of control.

In John 13, Jesus paints a picture
of the little church in the big world.
   The picture draws sharp contrasts:
In the world we live selfishly (guns and missiles).
In the church, we are to be servants (basin and towel).
   We are to lay down our lives for others!

"[Jesus] got up from the meal,
   took off his outer clothing,
      and wrapped a towel around his waist.
After that he poured water into a basin
   and began to wash his disciples' feet,
drying them with the towel
   that was wrapped around him." —John 13:4, 5

Peter protests, "You will never wash my feet!"

I confess that I find myself struggling in the mix—
   of being in the big world with its destructive forces,
versus my desire to be like Jesus
   and his small circle of followers.
There is selfishness in me that will not go away,
   the desire to reject the weak
      and those "others" not like myself.

I may associate "peace" with "weakness"
   and almost reject it as an option.
I like being wealthy and powerful.

In 1525, nearly 500 years ago,
   Mennonite forefathers and mothers
met in an upper room,
   in a hostile world
and talked about a new way of life.

They talked about "one anothering."
    Bless one another,
        Love one another,
            Pray for one another,
                Wash one another's feet.

This little band of believers
    found the Holy Scriptures
        to be about a New Way.

Finally, George Blaurach,
    one of the leaders in the group,
        asked to be baptized.
And one by one,
    others followed his example and were
baptized into the little family of faith.

We need to remember this rich beginning
    of the Anabaptist heritage.
Some of us belong to a church that has
    chosen to be distinctive and different.
We believe that God and his purpose will prevail
    and the world will find peace and harmony.

Back to John 13—
On that evening long ago

Jesus asks his disciples,
"Do you understand what I have done for you?
    Now that I . . . have washed your feet,
You also should wash one another's feet.
    I have set you an example
that you should do as I have done for you." —John 13:12, 14, 15

Jesus kneels before the disciples;
    he places himself at their disposal.
He comes without defenses;
    he is vulnerable, and available.
He takes the role of servant.

He asks us to be like him.
  "Lay down your life for your friend.
    Be vulnerable. Be available.
      Kneel before your fellow-believers.
        Put yourself at their disposal.
        Come without defenses.
          Risk all."

The world is very defensive
  and continues to embrace its own failing values.
Jesus tells us that if we are faithful,
  the world will hate us.
We are to be a contrast,
  and live in a New Way.
We wash each other's feet.
The basin and towel are important symbols for us.
  The world does not begin to understand this concept.

We yearn for a faithful church,
  but we do not yearn for the church alone.
We yearn for the world.
  Our mission is that the world may know
    and accept the New Way.

In the meantime, we wait
  and hold to the promise that "the kingdom of the world
  has become the kingdom of our Lord
    and of his Christ." —Revelation 11:15

Amen.

Credits

Note: The author has attempted to secure permission for telling stories of any persons named in this book. In some cases he has changed names to protect identities.

Kidd, Sue Monk. *When the Heart Waits: Spiritual Direction for Life's Sacred Questions.* San Franciso: HarperSan Francisco Publishers, 1992.

Buechner, Frederick. *A Room Called Remember.* San Francisco: Harper & Row, 1984.

Bonhoeffer, Dietrich. *Life Together.* San Francisco: HarperSan Francisco, 1993.

Gripe, Alan G. *The Interim Pastor's Manual.* Louisville, Ky.: Geneva Press, 1997.

Foster, Richard J. *Celebration of Discipline: The Path to Spiritual Growth.* San Francisco: HarperSan Francisco, 1998.

Hallie, Philip. *Lest Innocent Blood Be Shed.* New York: Harper & Row, 1979.

Lamott, Anne. *Traveling Mercies: Some Thoughts on Faith.* New York: Anchor Books, a division of Random House, Inc., 2000.

Longacre, Doris Janzen. *More-with-Less-Cookbook.* Scottdale, Pa.: Herald Press, 1976.

Meyer, Richard G. *One Anothering.* San Diego, Calif.: LuraMedia, 1990.

Nouwen, Henri J. M. *Life of the Beloved.* New York: Crossroads, 1992.

Peteson, Eugene H. *The Message/Remix.* Colorado Springs, Colo.: NavPress, 2002.

———. *The Jesus Way.* Grand Rapids, Mich.: Eerdmans, 2007.

Simpkinson, Charles and Anne, eds. *Sacred Stories.* San Francisco: HarperSan Francisco, 1993.

Willimon, William. *Worship as Pastoral Care.* Nashville: Abingdon Press, 1982.

The Author

Truman H. Brunk, retired pastor, lives in Harrisonburg, Virginia, with his wife Betty, a retired social worker. He considers himself "semi-retired," and stays semi-busy with his garden and sheep and fruit trees.

Through his living room window he watches the seasons change on the Massanutten Range, and through his dining room window he sees the mountains of West Virginia.

Sometimes he accepts invitations to speak in local churches. He likes to stay involved, with "a little preaching, a little writing, and a little interim work."

This is Truman's second book about his life and ministry. Brunk draws upon a lifetime of personal experiences with many age groups and people from a wide variety of backgrounds. He asks questions and does not always have the answers. He hopes the book will cause you to reflect on your own journey.

Truman believes that we need to listen and pay attention to what God is saying. We must open windows and catch God's message. The church is full of the disenfranchised, the weak, and the wounded who have no voice. Truman hopes he has ministered to the people on the fringe, helping them find their place at the table, and hear God's words of welcome.

The publication of his first book, *That Amazing Junk-Man* (Cascadia, 2007), opened up many opportunities for renewing old relationships and meeting new friends. Truman has been overwhelmed and blessed by letters and phone calls.

Book signings took on the atmosphere of family reunions. Sometimes at a book signing, Truman was asked to read aloud a chapter or two. At a signing in Dayton, Virginia, an older gentleman bought two copies of the book, one for himself and one for his pastor. In the following months, the newfound friend bought sixteen copies for family and friends!

Truman graduated from Eastern Mennonite College (now University) and Eastern Mennonite Seminary. He also studied at Union Theological Seminary in Richmond and in New York.

Since his ordination in 1965 and his twelve years as campus pastor at EMC, Truman has served as pastor in five locations: Akron Mennonite Church in Lancaster County, Pennsylvania; Blooming Glen Mennonite Church in Bucks County, Pennsylvania; Warwick River Mennonite Church in Newport News, Virginia; and associate pastor at Harrisonburg Mennonite Church in Harrisonburg, Virginia.

More recently he and Betty have served as interim pastors, including at Neffsville Mennonite Church and at Landisville Mennonite Church, both in Lancaster, Pennsylvania. Along with pastoral duties, Truman has been overseer for churches in Pennsylvania and Virginia.

Before his church work, Truman built houses in Newport News. In 1952 he married his childhood sweetheart, Elizabeth (Betty) Shenk. They are parents of two children: Kathleen, married to Dean Isaacs, lives near Raleigh, North Carolina, with their two young adult children, Andrew and Adrienne. Don, married to Deb Clemens, lives in Souderton, Pennsylvania, with son Isaac. Older son Caleb is married and lives nearby.

Reflecting on his life—working in the orchard, building homes, pastoring, everything—Truman would do it all again.

www.ingramcontent.com/pod-product-compliance
Ingram Content Group UK Ltd.
Pitfield, Milton Keynes, MK11 3LW, UK
UKHW041417180426
11947UKWH00007B/173